>> *Great Canadian* <<
Cookies, Bars
& Squares

>> Great Canadian << Cookies,

compiled by
SHEILA PEACOCK &
JENNIFER ABRAMS

CBC Radio listeners share
their family favourites

Bars & Squares

Douglas & McIntyre
VANCOUVER/TORONTO

Sheila: Thanks to my mom, who bakes exceptional treats. To my whole family, who love to devour her sweets. And to Sebastian Bear, who has finally decided to stop sleeping on top of the stove.

Jennifer: Thanks to my family, David, Ellen, Nancy and Joe. And thanks to my guinea pig, Barry.

Sheila and Jennifer would also like to thank Barbara Pulling, Robin Van Heck, Rob Sanders and all those at Douglas & McIntyre for their help, support and guidance. This project could not have happened without them.

This collection and introduction copyright © 2002 by Sheila Peacock, Jennifer Abrams and Canadian Broadcasting Corporation

Recipes copyright © 2002 by the authors

02 03 04 05 06   5 4 3 2 1

Douglas & McIntyre
2323 Quebec Street, Suite 201
Vancouver, British Columbia V5T 4S7
www.douglas-mcintyre.com

National Library of Canada Cataloguing in Publication Data

Main entry under title:

Great Canadian cookies, bars and squares

   Includes index.
   ISBN 1-55054-961-8

   1. Cookies. 2. Bars (Desserts) 3. Cookery, Canadian. I. Peacock, Sheila, 1964– II. Abrams, Jennifer, 1977–
TX772.G73 2002   641.8'654   C2002-910966-3

Editing by Robin Van Heck and Barbara Pulling
Cover design by Peter Cocking
Cover photograph by Alastair Bird/Alastair Bird Photography
Text design and typesetting by Gabi Proctor/DesignGeist
Printed and bound in Canada by Friesens
Printed on acid-free paper

The publisher gratefully acknowledges the financial support of the Canada Council for the Arts, the British Columbia Ministry of Tourism, Small Business and Culture, and the Government of Canada through the Book Publishing Industry Development Program (BPIDP) for its publishing activities.

A portion of the proceeds from the sale of this book will be donated to Big Brothers Big Sisters of Canada.

Contents

Introduction

Great Canadian Cookies, Bars and Squares started with a contest on CBC Radio One in British Columbia. We asked listeners for their all-time favourite cookie recipes and the stories behind them. In return, we offered CBC Radio fame for the winner, along with the latest celebrity cookbook. The response was tremendous. Dessert lovers everywhere rolled up their sleeves, dug into their family archives and sent in their sweetest offerings, each one accompanied by a story about what makes it special.

Before we knew it, we were baking all weekend to produce cookies for our hosts to judge on air. The resulting hour of stories and hilarity was a huge success, and a year later we decided to launch a second contest for favourite bar and square recipes. Some listeners had tried to sneak bars and squares into the cookie contest, so we knew there was an underground movement to give these popular treats their due. So many recipes were received and shared this time around that listeners lobbied for a cookbook. This collection represents our pick of the best.

In these pages, you'll find great Canadian cookies, bars and squares for every occasion. From nostalgic recipes passed down through generations to brand-new concoctions that will ensure fame in the family tree, there is something here for everybody's sweet tooth. All of the recipes have been fully tested, and their everyday ingredients and step-by-step instructions put them within easy reach of even occasional bakers. Because the accompanying stories celebrate families, sharing and childhood memories, we are donating a portion of the proceeds from sales of this book to Big Brothers Big Sisters of Canada.

The best desserts, like the best stories, are made for sharing. Whether you're celebrating with family, surprising your co-workers or simply having a good friend in for coffee, you'll find many wonderful possibilities in this collection of festive recipes from CBC Radio friends.

Sheila Peacock
Specials Producer for CBC Radio One & Two

Jennifer Abrams
CBC Radio

Chocolate Cookies, Bars and Squares

Nan's *Oh!* Bars

Brian Pace

This recipe came from my maternal grandmother, Zelma Blanche Jewers. A single mother of fifteen (my mother being the eldest), Nan was pregnant with her last child when her husband dropped dead of a heart attack. Endlessly resourceful, Nan sent the first five children away to work in the city; they would often send home their earnings to help raise their siblings. She served as the postmistress of the fishing village Ecum Secum, in Nova Scotia, for thirty-seven years.

I can remember running up the hill through my grandmother's amazing garden of giant, golden dinner-plate dahlias, roses and purple pansies. Her flowers were used for village weddings, parties and memorials at the graveyards. I'd help her with the endless weeding. These treats were her favourite snack, and we'd enjoy them with a cup of tea when we took a break from gardening.

In the Cottonwoods Community Garden in Strathcona, East Vancouver, I've built a memorial garden for my Nan. I collected those original dahlia bulbs and now grow them in my plot with rose bushes and other flowers. Curiously, I didn't plant purple pansies, yet they arrive every year. I make these Oh! Bars, then greet friends in the garden with them or just commune with the spirit of Nan. Her recipe uses ordinary ingredients, and yet, because of clever combinations, these bars are lifted above the ordinary. I think that is the trademark of a truly creative individual.

Makes 16 bars

Base

1/2 cup	butter
3/4 cup	white sugar
3 tbsp	honey
2	egg yolks
1/2 cup	milk
	zest and juice of 1 orange
1 1/2 cups	flour
1/2 tsp	salt
1 1/2 tsp	baking powder
1/2 cup	chocolate chips

Topping

2	egg whites
6 tbsp	brown sugar
	coconut to cover the meringue

Preheat the oven to 375°F.

Base: Cream the butter, white sugar, honey and egg yolks together. Add the remaining ingredients and mix together well. Spread in a greased 8-inch square baking pan and bake at 375°F for 25 to 30 minutes.

Topping: Beat the egg whites to form stiff peaks. Fold in the brown sugar. Remove the pan from the oven and spread the meringue on top of the base. Sprinkle liberally with coconut, covering the meringue. Return to the oven for 5 minutes to brown.

Cool on wire rack, cut bars and bliss out!

Hepcat Squares

Christina Symons

In 1974, my mom was still a hippie. She used to do embarrassing hippie things, including making hippie squares. Her favourite recipe was called "Wheat Germ Bars." The originals were dry as dust and coated with any kid's nemesis—melted carob chips. Over the years I convinced my mom that replacing the carob with chocolate would not compromise the healthiness of the squares. She had to agree—the chocolate improved the bars immensely.

Now it's 2002, and much to the chagrin of my mother, I'm a bit of a hippie myself. I still make wheat germ bars, using chocolate and a few additional ingredients for a creamier base. These are simple, light and tasty.

Makes 16 large squares

¹/₂ cup	butter, softened
¹/₂ cup	brown sugar, firmly packed
1 tsp	vanilla
1	egg
1 cup	all-purpose flour
¹/₂ cup	rolled oats
1 cup	wheat germ
¹/₂ cup	chocolate chips

Preheat the oven to 325°F.

Cream the butter and brown sugar until light. Beat in the vanilla and egg. Stir in the flour, oats and wheat germ. Press the mixture firmly into an ungreased 8-inch square baking pan. Bake at 325°F for 20 minutes.

Remove from the oven. Sprinkle the chocolate chips over the base and spread the chips when soft. Cool, then cut into squares.

Chocolate Rum Balls

Elizabeth Fleet

When we moved from Terrace to Castlegar, B.C., in 1980, I asked each of my friends to give me one of their favourite recipes. This one came from Inge Andrews. These are the best rum balls I have ever encountered. Every time I make them I laugh—not because of the essential sips of rum taken in the course of making them, but because of my first experience with the recipe. As I progressed through the instructions, I came to a part that said, "Sprinkle 3 tablespoons of rum and all of the milk over the dry ingredients." I recall that phone call to Inge: "Do you mean all of the milk in the fridge? All the milk you can spare? All the milk you can carry?" It was an excellent excuse to phone for a chat and a laugh with an old friend—and to find out that "all of the milk" was only one tablespoon!

Makes 30 rum balls

1 cup	ground almonds
1 cup	sifted icing sugar
1 tsp	instant coffee granules
3 squares	semi-sweet chocolate
1/3 cup	dark rum (divided)
1 tbsp	milk
	chocolate sprinkles to roll the balls in

Crush the coffee granules with the back of a teaspoon, so that they are powdered. Place the almonds in a large bowl and sift in the icing sugar and instant coffee. Grate the chocolate squares. (Machine grating with a fine blade is easiest, but the chocolate can also be grated by hand.) Stir the finely grated chocolate into the almond and sugar mixture. Sprinkle 3 tbsp of the rum and all of the milk over the dry ingredients. Stir until the mixture is evenly moistened and a uniform dark brown. Cover and chill for 10 minutes.

Remove from the refrigerator, shape into a ball and knead several times. Form the dough into 3/4-inch balls. (I use a rolling pin to roll the dough to about 3/4 inch thick, then cut the dough into small squares and shape them with my hands.) Dip the balls in the remaining rum, shake off any excess moisture and roll the balls in chocolate sprinkles. Place them on a cookie sheet to dry for about an hour. Store in an airtight container in a cool place. Let the rum balls "ripen" for a few days before serving, but not before sampling!

Dad's Brownies

Phil Claridge

In the early seventies, my wife and I were living in Thompson, Manitoba, where I worked for INCO (International Nickel). Marion Jasper, the wife of one of the fellows I was working with, sent these delicious brownies to the office, a Friday treat, I think. I asked for the recipe. When I got it, the icing part had been omitted, so I worked that out for myself. Greg and Marion left Thompson not long afterwards to return to Saskatchewan, and we have not communicated in a long time, but I still appreciate how generous Marion was to share such an excellent recipe. Although very stained, and ripped where it had been folded, the original sheet of dark-blue notepaper on which the recipe is written survives, and I still use it regularly. Our children call these "Dad's Brownies."

Makes 2 dozen brownies

3/4 cup	white sugar
1/2 cup	butter or margarine
2	eggs, slightly beaten
3 tbsp	unsweetened cocoa powder
1/2 cup	flour
1/2 cup	chopped walnuts
1 tsp	vanilla
3–4 cups	miniature marshmallows (to cover brownie base)

Icing

2 tbsp	butter or margarine
2 tbsp	unsweetened cocoa powder
1 1/2 tbsp	milk (skim is okay)
1/2 tsp	vanilla
3 1/2 cups	icing sugar

Preheat the oven to 350°F.

Cream together the white sugar and butter or margarine. Mix in the beaten eggs, cocoa, flour, walnuts and vanilla all at once. Batter will be stiff. Smooth it into a lightly greased 8- or 9-inch square pan. Bake at 350°F for about 20 minutes, removing the brownies from the oven before they are completely baked. Cover the brownies with a layer of the marshmallows and return the pan to the oven for about 4 to 5 minutes. The brownies will complete their baking and the marshmallows will melt together. Let the brownies cool while you prepare the icing.

Icing: In a double boiler, melt the butter or margarine and mix in the cocoa. Add the milk and vanilla. Keeping the double boiler on the heat, gradually beat in the icing sugar. To eliminate any lumps, continue to heat and beat the icing occasionally for 2 to 3 minutes after adding the last of the sugar. The icing will be quite runny but it will quickly set if you remove it from the heat or dribble some onto a cold plate. Drizzle the icing over the marshmallows so that it covers the top of the brownies. Don't try to spread the icing or it will lose its shiny appearance.

If you can, wait until the brownies are cool before cutting and removing them from the pan.

Christmas Brownies

Cindy Visser-DiCarlo

This recipe of my mother's is dear to my heart. She grew up in impoverished conditions, and childhood Christmases for her were very barren. She would tell me stories about how she was thrilled to find a Christmas orange in her stocking and how she would treasure the paper the orange came wrapped in. When my mother married and had two children of her own, she worked very hard with the little she and my father had to make our Christmases special.

One thing she always did was bake up a storm. There would be a gingerbread house decorated with candies and treats and at least eight different kinds of squares. My favourite was a chewy brownie topped with creamy mint icing. It was the first thing I would choose from the tray of dainties she set out for friends and family. Today, my oldest son also finds "those brownies with the mint icing" the best.

Makes 25 brownies

1 cup	sugar
2	eggs
1/2 cup	butter, melted
1/2 tsp	vanilla
1/2 cup	unsweetened cocoa powder
1/2 cup	flour
1/8 tsp	salt

Icing

1/4 cup	butter, softened
1 cup	icing sugar
2–3 tbsp	milk (or 1 egg yolk)
1/4 tsp	peppermint flavouring
1 drop	green food colouring (optional)
	chocolate shavings or sprinkles

Preheat the oven to 350°F.

Mix together the sugar, eggs, butter and vanilla. Add the dry ingredients, mixing well. Spoon the batter into a greased pan 7 x 11 inches, smooth out and bake at 350°F for 20 to 30 minutes. Test for doneness by inserting a wooden toothpick in centre of the pan— the toothpick should come out "clean," with no batter sticking to it. Cool the brownies.

Icing: Beat together the butter, icing sugar, milk or egg yolk, and peppermint flavouring. If you like, you can tint this icing a pale green with one drop of food colouring. Spread the icing on the cooled brownies. Shave chocolate onto the icing or top the icing with chocolate sprinkles.

Turtle Bars

Colleen Wells

I am married to a chocoholic. My husband, Mark, eats a chocolate treat every day. I created this special treat just for him, but I now make it for family and friends, and everybody likes it.

Makes 18 bars

Base

1 cup	pecans

Caramel centre

1 can	sweetened condensed milk (300 mL)
1/3 cup	white sugar
1/3 cup	butter
2 tbsp	corn syrup

Topping

4 squares	semi-sweet chocolate
1 tbsp	butter

Base: Spread the pecans on the bottom of an ungreased 8-inch square pan.

Caramel centre: Combine the milk, sugar, butter and corn syrup in a heavy saucepan. Cook and stir over low heat for 5 to 8 minutes, until the sugar is dissolved. Bring to a boil over medium heat and boil, stirring constantly, for 8 to 10 minutes or until the mixture thickens and turns a caramel colour. Spread over the pecans, then chill.

Topping: Melt the chocolate and butter, mix well, and spread over the cold caramel centre.

Charlotte's Chocolate Squares

Judy McCallum

This recipe was a favourite with my two sons when they were young. When they went to university, I frequently mailed portions to them. The cost of the postage would more than have paid for a nice chocolate cake from the local bakery, but it wouldn't have been the same. On one occasion, their dog managed to get to the parcel first, eating the envelope as well as the squares.

I owe this easy recipe to my cousin, Charlotte Nelson, who, like her mother and sisters, is a fabulous cook.

Makes 25 squares

3/4 cup	honey
1 cup	peanut butter
3 cups	Rice Krispies
1 cup	chocolate chips
1 tsp	vanilla
1 cup	salted peanuts

Mix the honey and peanut butter in a heavy saucepan. Heat on medium-high stirring constantly (it will burn easily) just until it starts to bubble. Remove from the heat and immediately mix in the Rice Krispies, chocolate chips, vanilla and peanuts. Press into a greased 8- or 9-inch square pan.

Tip: To measure peanut butter, butter or margarine, use a graduated 4-cup measuring cup. Fill it up to the one-cup mark with cold water and add the butter until the water level rises and indicates the correct amount required. Pour off the water and voila!

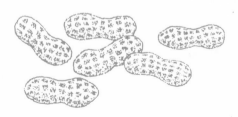

Rolo Cookies

Patti Kagawa

*W*hen I was young, this recipe was made only at Christmas. It is always special, because it takes some searching to find Rolos; they are not available at all stores. These cookies have wonderful caramel insides wrapped in chocolate and then covered in chewy cookie. Very delicious.

Makes 48 cookies

2 1/4 cups	flour
3/4 cup	unsweetened cocoa powder
1 tsp	baking soda
1 cup	white sugar
1 cup	brown sugar
1 cup	butter, softened
2	eggs
2 tsp	vanilla
1 cup	chopped pecans (divided)
1 tbsp	white sugar
48	Rolo candies (5 packages)

Preheat the oven to 350°F.

Combine the flour, cocoa and baking soda. Blend. In another bowl, combine 1 cup white sugar, 1 cup brown sugar and butter. Cream until fluffy, then add the eggs and vanilla. Add the flour mixture. Stir in 1/2 cup pecans.

With floured hands, shape cookies by wrapping 1 tbsp of dough completely around 1 Rolo. Combine the remaining 1/2 cup pecans and 1 tbsp sugar. Dip the balls in this. Place balls on an ungreased cookie sheet. Bake at 350°F until cracked on top (about 15 minutes).

White Chocolate Orange Dream Bars

John Mulloy

*C*reating something from scratch—squares, cookies or bars—may be part of the antidote to a disease many of us suffer from: time and meaning deficiency. Maybe if we made more things from start to finish, we'd slow down and remind ourselves of the natural order. Maybe we'd remember what we really need: a sense of fulfillment, of happiness, of peace.

Makes 6 dozen bars

1 cup	butter
2 cups	brown sugar, lightly packed
2	large eggs
2 tsp	vanilla
2 1/2 cups	all-purpose flour
1 tsp	baking soda
1/2 tsp	cinnamon
3 cups	rolled oats

Filling

1 can	sweetened condensed milk (300 mL)
1 1/2 cups	white chocolate chips
2 tbsp	butter
1 tbsp	grated orange zest
2/3 cup	pecans or almonds, chopped

Preheat the oven to 350°F. Grease a jelly-roll pan 10 x 15 inches and set it aside.

In a large bowl, cream 1 cup butter, sugar, eggs and vanilla until smooth and creamy.

Sift together the flour, baking soda and cinnamon. Gradually add this dry mixture to the creamed mixture and mix until smooth. Stir in the oats; set aside.

Filling: In a small saucepan, slowly heat the condensed milk, chocolate chips and 2 tbsp butter, stirring frequently, until smooth and melted. Stir in the orange zest and nuts.

Press two-thirds of the oat mixture into the prepared pan. Spread the chocolate filling evenly over the base. Sprinkle the remaining oat mixture evenly on top.

Bake at 350°F for 25 to 30 minutes or until golden. Cool and cut into bars.

Bertha's Amazing Chocolate Cranberry Cookies

Kathryn Brisco

These cookies are in demand at every family gathering. My mother-in-law, Bertha, makes at least a double batch as a small component of her Christmas baking. My husband's family holds a Christmas nativity pageant in their backyard every year. The children dress up as angels, wise men, innkeepers and the like. The adults are the audience, intermittently drinking hot liquids, eating cookies and singing carols.

Makes 3 dozen cookies

1 cup	butter
1 cup	brown sugar
1 cup	white sugar
2	eggs
1 tsp	vanilla
2 1/2 cups	rolled oats, ground
2 cups	all-purpose flour
1 tsp	baking powder
1 tsp	baking soda
1/2 tsp	salt
2 cups	chocolate chips
1 1/2 cups	dried cranberries
1 cup	shredded coconut

Preheat the oven to 375°F.

Cream the butter and sugars. Blend in the eggs and vanilla. Using a grinder or food processor, finely grind the oats.

Combine the ground oats, flour, baking powder, baking soda and salt in separate bowl. Add to the creamed mixture gradually. Stir in the chocolate chips, cranberries and coconut. Drop heaping tablespoonfuls onto a greased baking sheet. If the baking sheet is thin, line it with foil (dull side up).

Bake the cookies at 375°F for 10 to 12 minutes. They should be light in colour—do not overbake them. This recipe can be doubled (and usually is).

Triple Chocolate Oatmeal Orange Spice Cookies

Ken Fabok

Fifteen centuries before Cortez, a distant relative of mine was shipwrecked in a rich and vibrant land where the stars were strange and the weather was never cold. How this relative returned to northern Europe is a matter of myth and legend, but for many centuries there survived recipes in Latin and a strange form of hieroglyphic writing. All of the recipes included chocolate, oranges, allspice and vanilla. They evolved over the centuries into various cakes and confections. One of them is this biscuit. It tastes best served on the winter solstice, when the night is longest.

Makes 12 to 18 cookies

3¹/3 cups	all-purpose or whole wheat flour
2¹/2 tsp	baking soda
1¹/2 tsp	baking powder
¹/2 tsp	salt
6 heaping tbsp	unsweetened cocoa powder (dark)
	grated zest from 3 medium or 2 large hard, thick-skinned oranges
2 generous cups	mixed chocolate chips
1 lb	butter or margarine
2 cups	golden sugar, packed
2	large eggs
4 tbsp	orange juice
5 tsp	vanilla
1 tsp	cloves or allspice
1 heaping tbsp	cinnamon
2 ²/3 cups	cooking oats, ground in a food processor
	grated hard dark chunk chocolate for topping (optional)

Preheat the oven to 350°F.

Whisk the baking soda, baking powder and salt into the flour. Sift the cocoa into the flour mixture. Add the grated orange zest and mixed chocolate chips into the flour mixture and mix well. (I like to use a mixture of regular-sized dark premium chocolate chips and white chocolate chips with jumbo milk chocolate chips.)

In a larger bowl, beat the butter on medium speed until creamy. Add the golden sugar, eggs, orange juice, vanilla, cloves or allspice, and cinnamon and beat until well blended.

Stir the flour mixture into the butter mixture with rubber spatula until well blended. Usually I slip on a clean rubber glove and mix by hand. Add the ground cooking oats to mixture. Here you really have to use your hands!

Taking larger-than-golf-ball–sized amounts of dough, flatten each into a cookie shape and place on a greased cookie sheet. If you like, grate some hard dark chunks of chocolate and add this as a nice topping before the cookies go into the oven.

Bake in a preheated 350°F oven for 10 minutes on the lower-middle rack (this is my electric oven standard). Make sure you use a timer. (With some ovens, the cookies may take a bit longer—perhaps as much as 15 minutes, but this is the maximum and you will need to watch them carefully.)

Mocha Hazelnut Nanaimo Bars

Lisa Noble

Our annual Christmas bakeathon began when its other two founders, Mary Frances and Sara, were students with me at the University of Ottawa. MF, as she is known to those who love her, is one of those people who should have been born a grandma. When Sara and I trekked home from the market on wet or snowy Saturday mornings, there would be fresh gingersnaps (from MF's grandma's recipe) and freshly brewed tea awaiting us. One year, MF and Sara suggested that we save money on gifts by baking up a storm of cookies and squares, splitting them three ways and then giving them away. From economic necessity comes great things.

All these years later, Sara lives in Calgary (although we usually call her during the bakeathon), and Rebekah and Alice have often joined us in her stead. Our "cookie weekend" in December has seen us through marriages, divorces, new houses, family health crises and much more. My eight-month-old son was the first child to join us (although his father was charged with keeping him out of the kitchen, where the knives and hot cookie sheets were flying). We always start on a Friday afternoon by preparing the slice-and-bake doughs that need to be refrigerated (or left out on an Ottawa porch) overnight, and these are the first to be baked on Saturday morning. Last year, by the time the Chinese takeout arrived for Saturday supper, there were approximately 1,800 cookies and squares packed into tins for four bakers to take home and distribute to eager recipients.

Some of our recipes change from year to year, but we would be in very big trouble if we were to eliminate this one. The recipe looks like a lot of work, but it's decidedly worth it. These have been praised by the people I teach with as a better way to start the day than a large Tim's double-double, and they have earned me marriage proposals from the baggage checkers at Toronto's Union Station, who insisted on knowing what was in the heavy backpack that clanked. Warning: Cut these small—they are deadly!

Makes 32 bars

Base

1 1/2 cups	graham wafer crumbs
1 cup	flaked sweetened coconut
1/2 cup	finely chopped toasted hazelnuts
2/3 cup	butter
1/3 cup	unsweetened cocoa powder
1/4 cup	white sugar
1 tbsp	instant coffee granules (Alice insists these must not be decaf!)
1	egg, lightly beaten

Filling

2 cups	icing sugar
1/4 cup	butter, softened
1 tbsp	instant coffee granules
2 tbsp	water

Topping

2 tbsp	butter
1 tbsp	instant coffee granules
4 oz	semi-sweet chocolate, coarsely chopped

Preheat the oven to 350°F. Grease an 8-inch square cake pan and set it aside.

Base: In a large bowl, stir together the graham wafer crumbs, coconut and hazelnuts; set aside. In a saucepan, heat the butter, cocoa, sugar and coffee granules over low heat, stirring until the butter is melted. Remove from the heat and whisk in the egg. Stir in the crumbs until well mixed. Press this mixture evenly into the prepared pan; bake in the centre of 350°F oven for 10 minutes. Cool the base (in pan) completely on a rack (or put it out on your porch, if it's cold enough and you have no squirrels to contend with).

Filling: In a bowl, beat half of the icing sugar with the 1/4 cup butter. Mix the coffee granules with 2 tbsp water; beat into the butter mixture along with the remaining icing sugar. Spread the filling over the cooled base.

Topping: In a heatproof bowl set over a saucepan of hot (not boiling) water, melt the butter with the coffee granules; add the chocolate and stir until melted and smooth. Let the topping cool slightly before spreading it over the filling.

Chill in the refrigerator (or back on the porch) for about 2 hours or until the chocolate is firm. Let the bars stand at room temperature for 5 minutes to soften slightly before you cut them.

Wrapped well, these bars will be fine in the refrigerator for a week, or in the freezer for 2 weeks. The recipe doubles extremely well to fill a pan 9 x 13 inches.

Marpole Bars

Warren Flett

I like to take the recipes I have gathered and customize them. This is how "Marpole Bars" were born. They resemble Nanaimo Bars in appearance, but their flavour is unique. The Oreo crumbs give them a full, rich flavour, the coffee adds a West Coast buzz and the white chocolate tops everything off with a touch of decadence. What makes this recipe among the best in the land? Friends on four different continents—from Canada and the U.S. to England, South Africa and Australia—have requested it.

Makes 16 to 18 bars

Bottom layer

¹/₃ cup	butter or margarine
¹/₃ cup	sugar
1 tsp	vanilla
2	eggs, beaten
3 cups	Oreo crumbs or crushed chocolate wafers

Middle layer

¹/₄ cup	butter or margarine
1 tbsp	finely ground coffee
¹/₂ tsp	vanilla
2 cups	icing sugar
¹/₂ cup	milk

Top layer

2 tbsp	butter or margarine
3–4 squares	white baking chocolate, chopped

CBC baker's note: Oreo crumbs are sold in the baking section of grocery stores where you would also find graham wafer crumbs. However, if your local store doesn't have them, you can substitute plain dark chocolate wafers and crush them yourself. Crushing whole Oreo cookies is not recommended, because you would also have the Oreo icing mixed in, which would drastically change the texture of the crust.

Bottom layer: Melt the butter in a saucepan over low heat (don't burn it!). Add the sugar. Remove from the heat and whisk in the vanilla and eggs. Add the cookie crumbs and mix thoroughly. Press the crumb mixture into an 8- or 9-inch square pan (depending on the thickness of crust you prefer). Put into the refrigerator or freezer to cool.

Middle layer: Cream the butter in a mixing bowl. Stir in the ground coffee and vanilla. Add small amounts of the icing sugar and milk alternately, mixing well after each addition, until all of the icing sugar is used and the mixture is quite thick. When the bottom layer is cool, spread the middle layer over it and put the pan back into refrigerator to set.

Top layer: In the microwave, melt the butter and pieces of white chocolate on medium power (50 per cent) for about 2 minutes or until the chocolate is completely melted. (If you don't have a microwave, place the butter and chocolate in a double boiler, or in a glass bowl over a saucepan of boiling water—don't let the water touch the bottom of the bowl. Heat the butter and chocolate until melted, then remove from the heat. *Never* put a glass bowl directly on a hot stove-top element.) Whisk the butter and chocolate together thoroughly and pour on top of cold, set middle layer. Shake the pan around until the chocolate is evenly distributed. Refrigerate the pan again to set the top layer.

Keep the bars refrigerated until you are ready to cut and serve them.

Queen of the Nanaimo Bars

Dean Nixon

Sometime in the mid-1940s, my parents left Victoria and settled in Vancouver. Somehow my mother, Christina Nixon, obtained a recipe clipped from a Nanaimo, B.C., newspaper. That's why we called this a "Nanaimo Bar"—it originated with that newspaper recipe.

Mom was the only one in our family, or in her social circle, to make this confection, and she developed a reputation for it. For family events, dinner parties and potluck suppers, she was always asked to make her Nanaimo Bars. When I was little, she asked what I wanted served at my birthday party. I replied, without a moment's hesitation, "Some of that really keen junk!"—meaning, of course, Nanaimo Bars. We moved to Toronto in 1958, and Mom's Nanaimo Bar reputation took off there, too. Nobody in the east had ever seen such a thing, and at first bite they were conquered and converted.

I think it was in the late 1970s that I first saw a commercially produced Nanaimo Bar. I was floored. How could this be? How did our secret get out? Had someone copied my Mom's recipe? Were there other families out there somewhere who had held the Nanaimo Bar as a treasured "family secret"? Had the recipe been produced in a cookbook? I never learned the answer to those questions.

Now the Nanaimo Bar is everywhere. But none of the commercial bars are as good as my Mom's. The yellow middle layer is too sugary-sweet and has too gooey a texture. They never put enough walnuts or shredded coconut in the bottom layer, either. My Mom was eighty-three when she began to slide down the slippery slope of failing health. The last year she attempted her usual Christmas baking, it was a disaster. That was a sad and poignant Christmas for us all. Mom was frustrated with herself and the rest of us mourned the gradual erosion of this once vital and vibrant woman. We also mourned the loss of a family tradition. We would never again taste Mom's wonderful Nanaimo Bars.

Mom died three years later. We published her recipe for Nanaimo Bars in her memorial service program, and we served them up (homemade, of course) at the reception following the service.

May the Force be with you, and may the true Nanaimo Bar rule the galaxy.

Makes 9 to 12 bars

Bottom layer

1/2 cup	butter, softened
1/4 cup	sugar
5 tbsp	unsweetened cocoa powder
1 tsp	vanilla
1	egg, beaten
1 3/4 cups	graham wafer crumbs
1 cup	shredded coconut
1/2 cup	chopped walnuts

Middle layer

1/4 cup	butter, softened
3 tbsp	milk
2 tbsp	vanilla custard powder
2 cups	icing sugar

Top layer

4 squares	semi-sweet chocolate
1 tbsp	butter

Bottom layer: Place the softened butter, sugar, cocoa, vanilla and egg in a bowl. Set over boiling water and stir until the butter melts and the mixture resembles custard. In a separate bowl, combine the graham crumbs, coconut and walnuts, blending well. Add to the custard-like mixture. Press evenly into a greased 9-inch pan. Cool to set.

Middle layer: Mix the butter, milk, custard powder and icing sugar thoroughly and spread over the cooled bottom layer.

Top layer: Melt the chocolate with the butter. When it is cool but still liquid, pour and spread over the middle layer.

Chill the Nanaimo Bars in the refrigerator.

Coconut Cookies, Bars and Squares

Cherry Chews

Shannon Macdonald

My grandma's recipe book is black, well used and has a musty smell. It is deceivingly plain. The leather cover is worn through at the corners. But this book is magic. Lift the cover and time stops.

All of the recipes on the yellowed pages are written out in perfectly formed handwriting, and almost all have a date and an origin noted: Pauline's Cheese Crunchies (Penticton, 1976); Hard Sauce (Vancouver Sun, 1960); Christmas Punch (Grand Forks, 1973). On some, Gram has made extra little notes to herself: "Try walnuts instead." "Peg's wedding cake." "Delicious!"

Lola Macdonald passed away in September of 2000, and this black book is now my treasured possession. It is more than a cookbook. It is a book alive with stories and people.

Makes 12 to 16 squares

Base

1 cup	flour
1 cup	rolled oats
1 cup	brown sugar
1 tsp	baking soda
1/4 tsp	salt
1/2 cup	butter

Filling

2	eggs
1 cup	brown sugar
1/2 tsp	almond extract
2 tbsp	flour
1/2 tsp	baking powder
1/2 tsp	salt
1 cup	coconut
1 cup	maraschino cherries, drained and quartered
1/2 cup	pecan halves

Icing

3 tbsp	butter, softened
2 cups	icing sugar
1/4 tsp	almond extract
2 tbsp	liquid from the maraschino cherries

Preheat the oven to 350°F.

Base: Mix together the flour, oats, brown sugar, baking soda and salt. Add the butter and mix until crumbly, first with a fork, then with your fingers. Press into a greased 8-inch square baking pan and bake for 10 minutes at 350°F.

Filling: Beat the eggs, then stir in the brown sugar and almond extract. Sift together the flour, baking powder and salt, and stir into the egg mixture. Add the coconut and cherries, and stir to blend. Pour over the base and spread evenly. Sprinkle with the pecans and bake at 350°F for 45 minutes. Let cool.

Icing: Blend the butter and icing sugar. Add the almond extract and enough liquid from the cherries to make the icing spreadable. Ice the squares when they have cooled.

Grammi's Fantastic Lemon Squares

Linda Scales

These squares are delicious and easy to make, and they bring back warm memories of my Grandmother MacAusland, who would have a pan ready for me when I visited her in Bloomfield, P.E.I., as a child. I love the intense lemon taste of the smooth, creamy filling and the crunchiness of the toasted coconut on top. As an adult, I have made these for friends many times, and they rave about them, too.

Makes 16 to 20 squares

Base

1/2 cup	butter
1/2 cup	white sugar
1	whole egg
2	egg yolks
1/2 cup	flour
3/4 tsp	baking powder
1/2 tsp	vanilla
1/8 tsp	salt

Filling

1 can	sweetened condensed milk (300 mL)
2	lemons, juice and grated zest

Topping

2	egg whites
1 cup	white sugar
1/2 cup	coconut

Base: Preheat the oven to 350°F. Cream the butter and sugar together. Beat the egg and egg yolks; add to the butter mixture and cream together. Stir in the flour, baking powder, vanilla and salt. Mix thoroughly. Pat into a greased 8-inch square baking pan. Bake at 350°F for about 9 to 10 minutes—it should be a very light colour and if you press down lightly in the middle with the tip of your finger, it should leave a small dent. Do not overcook! Cool the base.

Filling: Preheat the oven again to 350°F. Beat the sweetened condensed milk with the juice and grated zest of the lemons. Pour the filling onto the cooled base, smoothing it evenly to the edges.

Topping: Beat the egg whites, adding the sugar gradually until the meringue is foamy and moist. Spoon it on top of the filling and spread it to the edges of the pan. Sprinkle the coconut all over the top. Bake at 350°F until the meringue is lightly browned—how long this will take depends on the oven so keep your eye on it; it could take anywhere from 5 to 10 minutes.

Let cool before cutting into squares and eating. (CBC baker's note: These delicate squares do not travel well once cut. If you're taking them elsewhere to be eaten, take the whole pan and cut them at your destination.)

Tante Bag Cookies

cb meijers

Tante Bag was my aunt, my mom's sister. Her full name was Balligje (a very old-fashioned Dutch name), but everyone called her "Bag" (it rhymes with "yuchhh"). Tante Bag, like many other women of her time, emigrated to Canada to marry her fiancé, who had gone ahead to "set up" in hopes of a good and prosperous life in those postwar years. She and her husband went on to have five children.

Although times were tough and money was tight, no self-respecting Dutch person would ever have a cup of coffee without some kind of biscuit or pastry. This is still true today. In Dutch cafés, a small cookie accompanies every coffee sold. Tante Bag's recipe was born of desperation to make something presentable from the ingredients at hand. The result has become a famous and regular part of our baking repertoire.

Makes 2 dozen cookies

Base

1 cup	white sugar
2/3 cup	butter
2 cups	flour
1 tsp	almond extract
2 tsp	baking powder
4	egg yolks

Meringue

4	egg whites
1 cup	brown sugar
1 cup	shredded, sweetened coconut

Preheat the oven to 325°F.

Base: Mix the sugar, butter, flour, almond extract, baking powder and egg yolks into a dry but consistent crumble. Distribute evenly on big cookie sheet and flatten lightly with the palm of your hand.

Meringue: Whip the egg whites until they form stiff peaks. Fold in the brown sugar and coconut. Spread the meringue mixture on top of the cookie base.

Bake at 325°F for 30 minutes or until barely browned— lighter is better. Let cool. Cut into squares with a wet knife.

These cookies keep well for a long time when frozen, but separate layers of them with waxed paper.

Pink Sin

Betty Anne Malloff

I first tasted these squares at Pleasant Park Public School in Ottawa in the early eighties, when I was an itinerant music teacher. I thought I had died and gone to heaven! They are truly decadent, as a good square should be. I don't make them very often, but they are a favourite with family, friends and workmates. I even got a Christmas card from a friend saying how much he missed Pink Sin (hint, hint). The secret is in the icing. Some people guess that it is cream cheese since the texture is so different and creamy. For best results, be sure to beat the icing for two minutes after each addition.

Makes 2 to 3 dozen squares

Base

1 cup	graham wafer crumbs
1/2 cup	butter, melted
1/2 cup	brown sugar
1 heaping tsp	flour

Middle layer

2 cups	coconut
1 can	sweetened condensed milk (300 mL)

Icing

1/2 cup	butter, softened (not melted)
3/4 cup	icing sugar
2 tbsp	cream or milk
2 tbsp	boiling water
few drops	red food colouring
1/2 tsp	vanilla

Base: Preheat the oven to 375°F. Mix together the graham wafer crumbs, melted butter, brown sugar and flour. Press into a greased 8-inch square pan and bake at 375°F for 5 to 10 minutes. Cool.

Middle layer: Preheat the oven to 350°F. Mix together the coconut and condensed milk, then spread on the cooled base. Bake at 350°F for 15 to 20 minutes, or until gold around the edges. Cool thoroughly.

Icing: Note that after each addition, you must beat for 2 minutes. Start by beating the butter for 2 minutes. Add the icing sugar and again beat for 2 minutes. Add the cream or milk and beat for 2 more minutes. Add the boiling water and beat for 2 minutes. Add the food colouring and, you got it, beat for 2 minutes. Lastly, add the vanilla and beat for 2 more minutes. Spread the icing over cooled squares.

Keep the squares in the refrigerator.

Mrs. French's Pineapple Squares

Deb Calderon

I love collecting old cookbooks. They have such wonderful recipes. This one comes from a cookbook featuring favourite recipes of the ladies of the Drumheller Salvation Army Home League and their friends. When I make these squares, I often wonder who Mrs. Alys French was and what her life was like.

Makes 16 to 18 squares

Base

1 cup	flour
1/2 cup	butter
1/2 cup	brown sugar

Filling

2	beaten eggs
1 cup	brown sugar
4 tbsp	flour
1/2 tsp	baking powder
1/8 tsp	salt
1/2 cup	coconut
1 cup	crushed pineapple, drained

Base: Preheat the oven to 400°F. Mix the flour, butter and brown sugar until crumbly, then pat down in a well-greased 8-inch square baking pan. Bake at 400°F for 10 minutes. Let cool.

Filling: Preheat the oven to 350°F. Mix together the beaten eggs, brown sugar, flour, baking powder, salt, coconut and pineapple. Pour the filling ingredients onto the cooled crust. Bake at 350°F for 20 to 25 minutes, or until well browned.

These squares may be served with or without a plain icing.

Hello Dollies

Ann E. Sullivan

Hello Dollies are, without a doubt, my favourite bars. If you asked my sisters and my brother, my cousins and my dad, I think their answers would be the same. Just the thought of that combination of gooey chocolate, butterscotch chips and coconut layered on a graham-wafer crust and smothered with sweetened condensed milk gets me all misty-eyed.

Even more than their taste, it's the memories Hello Dollies evoke that make them so special to me. They are a Sullivan tradition. My mom made Hello Dollies every Christmas—and only at Christmas, so they were definitely a treat. As kids, we fought over the chance to cut them into bars because that meant we could eat the resulting crumbs. Hello Dollies were always the first thing to disappear, long before the chewy date balls, the mincemeat squares or the fruitcake.

My mom died when I was eighteen, but she would be happy to know that her children (and even her husband, who swears he can't make "pastries") are carrying on her Hello Dollies tradition. Each of us makes a slightly different version. This recipe is for the basic bars, but it's fun to experiment: dress them up with red and green dried fruit, use more (way more!) chocolate than is called for, skip the nuts or the coconut, replace the butterscotch chips with Skor pieces, or bake them in a smaller pan for thicker bars.

Makes 4 dozen bars

1/2 cup	butter
1 1/2 cups	graham wafer crumbs
1 cup	shredded coconut
1 cup	chocolate chips
1 cup	butterscotch chips
1 can	sweetened condensed milk (300 mL)
1 cup	chopped nuts

Preheat the oven to 350°F.

Melt the butter in a baking pan 9 x 13 inches. Sprinkle the graham wafer crumbs evenly over the melted butter and press down. Next sprinkle on the coconut, then the chocolate chips and butterscotch chips. Pour the condensed milk evenly over all. Sprinkle the nuts on top and press down lightly. Bake at 350°F for 30 minutes. Cool in the pan on a wire rack.

Grandma White's Thimble Cookies, 1947

Judy White

This recipe was my grandmother's first, then it was passed on to my mother and to me. That fact alone would make it special. But there's the added attraction of these cookies being quick and very easy to make, with few ingredients necessary. They seem never to fail. They also never fail to draw rave reviews from tasters, who always want the recipe. Since we operate a small B&B inn in the middle of Okanagan orchard country, these are a great way to show off our homemade apricot jam.

Makes 1 dozen cookies

1/2 cup	butter
1/4 cup	brown sugar
1	egg yolk, well beaten
1 cup	flour
1 tsp	baking powder
1 tsp	vanilla
1	egg white, beaten
Several tbsp	long-thread coconut
1/3 cup	jam (your favourite)

Preheat the oven to 350°F.

Mix together, in order, the butter, brown sugar, egg yolk, flour, baking powder and vanilla. Roll pieces of the dough into walnut-sized balls. Dent the top of each ball with a thimble (or fingertip). Dip the tops into the beaten egg white and then into the coconut and place on an ungreased cookie sheet.

Bake at 350°F for 15 minutes. Remove from the oven and dent the tops again. Return to the oven and bake another 10 minutes. Remove from the oven and fill the dent in each cookie with jam.

5-in-1 Bars

Joan Fraser

This recipe was given to me many, many years ago by a neighbour. She was an elderly lady who taught the game of bridge to young mothers in the neighbourhood. While our kids were in kindergarten, we'd meet at her house. She served tea and 5-in-1 Bars and graced us with a lesson in bridge, all for 25 cents! It was that long ago.

I have made these bars constantly ever since—they are a great treat. And the recipe is a cinch.

Makes approximately 20 bars

1 cup	butter, softened
1 cup	brown sugar, lightly packed
1 cup	oats
1 cup	finely shredded coconut
1 cup	flour

Preheat the oven to 350°F.

Blend all of the ingredients until crumbly. Spread in an ungreased 8-inch square baking pan and press it down with your fingers until it is ¼–½ inch thick. Bake at 350°F for 15 to 20 minutes, until lightly brown. Cut into bars while still hot.

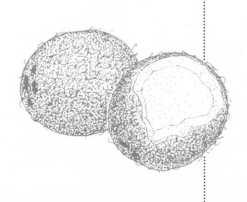

First Snow Cookies

Leslie Rowlands

When dusted with icing sugar, these cranberry cookies remind me of the first snowfall of the season. I used to use red and green glacé cherries in them, but in a move to healthier baking I now substitute dried cranberries. The cookie-dough logs can be frozen ahead, then brought out, sliced and baked for instant sparkle any time during the holidays. When my kids were at home and wanted to help with Christmas baking, I just gave them the logs to work from—no kitchen mess! The logs also make great gifts when wrapped in waxed paper and cellophane. Best of all, these cookies are easy to make and pack lots of cranberry punch. You can also add tiny chocolate chips, or use a dash of your favourite liquor instead of almond extract if you like.

Makes 64 cookies

1 cup	butter
3/4 cup	sugar
5 tbsp	milk
2 tsp	almond extract
1 1/2 cups	flour
3/4 cup	dried cranberries, chopped
1/3 cup	finely chopped pecans
1/2 cup	unsweetened shredded coconut
	icing sugar for dusting the cookies

Cream the butter with the sugar until fluffy. Add the milk and almond extract. Add the flour and beat until smooth. Stir in the dried cranberries and pecans. Turn the dough onto a floured board and, adding a little flour if needed, pat into two 8-inch logs. Roll the logs in the coconut, then wrap them in waxed paper and chill in the refrigerator for a couple of hours.

To bake the cookies, preheat the oven to 350°F. Remove one log from the refrigerator and cut just enough 1/4-inch slices to fill a cookie sheet lined with parchment paper. (Keep the rest of the log refrigerated between trayings.) Bake at 350°F for 10 minutes or until the edges of the cookies are lightly browned. Remove and cool on a rack. Dust lightly with icing sugar when cool.

Crunchies

Melanie Kalley

As far back as I can recall from my childhood in South Africa, my mother made these squares, for three very good reasons:

1. *They are absolutely delicious—everyone loves them.*
2. *They are so quick to make. You have fresh squares in about 20 minutes— no sifting, no kneading, no rolling, no fuss.*
3. *They require no unusual or expensive ingredients.*

My mother was not a "stay-at-home" mother, and she was often too tired in the evening to bake. My brother, Kevin, at age eight, took matters into his own hands. He found the recipe book and taught himself to bake these squares. From that time on, there were always Crunchies in the house.

Makes 4 dozen squares

1 cup	flour
1 cup	sugar
1 cup	quick-cooking oats
1 cup	unsweetened coconut
1/4 lb	butter or margarine
1/2 tsp	baking soda
3 tbsp	golden corn syrup

Preheat the oven to 350°F.

Mix the flour, sugar, oats and coconut together in a bowl. In a saucepan, melt the butter, baking soda and golden syrup together over low heat (do not use a microwave). Add the butter mixture to the dry ingredients and mix well. Press the dough evenly into a greased cookie sheet (12 x 18 inches).

Bake at 350°F for 12 to 15 minutes or until it turns golden brown (watch carefully as it tends to burn easily). Cut into squares immediately after removing the sheet from the oven. Allow the squares to cool slightly on the tray (until they begin to firm up), then remove them to a cooling rack.

Xakanaxa Game Farm Cookies

Hilda Stanger

Two years ago, at the Xakanaxa (pronounced Kakanaka) Game Farm in Botswana's Moremi Wildlife Reserve, we had our most splendid Christmas ever—an elaborate Victorian dinner complete with candelabra, crackers, turkey dinner and Bob's special pickles. We went on game drives during the early morning and at dusk, and on boat rides in the seas of grass during the day. These are the cookies we had for tea and elevensies, and they are the best I've ever had—take it from a non–cookie-lover. We were told this was a special secret family recipe. Even Amadeus, the friendly hippo, didn't know it.

Makes 3 dozen cookies

1 cup	margarine
1 cup	white sugar
1 cup	brown sugar
2	eggs
2 tsp	vanilla
2 cups	flour
1 tsp	baking soda
1/8 tsp	salt
1 cup	coconut
2 cups	oats
2 cups	bran flakes cereal, crushed

Preheat the oven to 350°F.

Cream the margarine and sugars together. Add the eggs and vanilla. Sift and fold in the flour, soda and salt. Stir in the coconut, oats and crushed bran flakes.

Shape the dough into small balls and place on an ungreased cookie sheet. Bake at 350°F for 10 minutes.

Fruit Cookies, Bars and Squares

Raisin Squares

Laurie Auger

This is a recipe created by my mother sometime in the late fifties or early sixties to accommodate her youngest daughter (me) who could not abide dates or date squares. Mom was very creative in the kitchen—she had to be, especially during the thirties and into the war years, when everything was scarce or beyond our means. For several years, I am told, she did not even have an oven, just a hot plate for which my father devised a metal hood of some sort so that Mom could bake her bread. Everything she made, she made from scratch. In my innocent youth I actually envied some of my friends their frozen TV dinners and chocolate instant pudding pies. Now I know better.

The following recipe is messy, sweet and delicious. This is one square that is almost impossible to eat with your hands, so sit down at the table with a plate and a fork to enjoy it.

Makes 16 to 18 squares

Base and topping

1 1/3 cups	flour
1 1/3 cups	brown sugar, lightly packed
1/2 tsp	baking soda
1 1/3 cups	rolled oats (not that horrible quick or instant stuff!)
2/3 cup	butter, melted

Filling

2 cups	seedless raisins
2 cups	water
1/2–2/3 cup	sugar
2 tbsp	flour
1/2 tsp	vanilla
1 tbsp	butter
1 tbsp	lemon juice

Base and topping: Mix together the flour and brown sugar. Stir in the baking soda and rolled oats. With a fork, blend in the melted butter.

Press about half to two-thirds of this crust stuff into the bottom of an 8- or 9-inch square pan. (I suggest the smaller amount.)

Filling: Simmer the raisins and water together. Mix the sugar and flour and gently stir this into the raisin mixture. Cook gently until it is quite thick. (Again, using the smaller amount of sugar works well.) Blend in the vanilla, butter and lemon juice. Let this filling cool off a little.

Preheat the oven to 350°F. Pour the cooled filling over the crust in the pan. Top the filling with the remaining oats mixture and press the oats down firmly. Bake at 350°F for 30 to 35 minutes, until it is a lovely golden brown.

Let it cool before you cut it into squares.

Baba's Raisin-Surprise Cookies

Jan Pawlik

Being an avid cook and baker, I remember the people in my life who over the years gave me the desire to learn and the secrets they shared in their baking. Many of them have passed away now, and many memories are captured in the recipes I've collected. Baba (Clara) passed on in August 1999, but her love of baking and the time she spent in the kitchen will live on in our hearts forever. This recipe is submitted in memory of her.

Makes approximately 3 dozen cookies

Cookie dough

1 cup	butter, softened
2 cups	brown sugar, packed
1 tsp	pure vanilla
3 cups	white flour
1 tsp	baking soda
1 tsp	salt

Filling

1/2 cup	white sugar
1/2 cup	water
1 1/2 cups	raisins
1 tbsp	butter
1 tbsp	lemon juice
1 tbsp	cornstarch

Cookie dough: Mix all of the ingredients together until they are well blended and the dough is smooth in texture. Put aside while making the filling.

Filling: Gently boil together the sugar and water. Add the raisins and simmer for about 5 minutes, until the raisins plump up. Then add the butter and lemon juice, mixed with the cornstarch, stirring until the mixture is thickened. Let cool.

To bake the cookies, preheat the oven to 350°F. Using 2 teaspoons, drop pieces of dough onto a well-greased cookie sheet. Indent each with your fingertip, creating a little well in the middle of the cookie dough. Place a dollop (about 1/2 tsp) of filling in the well, then cover the filling with more cookie dough (about 1/2 tsp). Bake at 350°F for 10 to 20 minutes, until golden brown.

Lebkuchen

Ruth Tubbesing

Ten years ago I wanted some traditional cookie recipes from the German side of my origins, and I asked a friend if her friend in Bavaria could share a few with me. The Bavarian woman referred me to a friend of hers who lived in Richmond, B.C. This lady kindly agreed to meet me in a café, where she dictated several recipes while we drank coffee and ate cake. She moved shortly after that, and I was never able to contact her again. If she is reading this, I'd like to say thank you. From my handwritten notes, along with little improvements added from experience, here is my recipe for Lebkuchen. It is very easy.

Makes 30 cookies

2	whole eggs
1 cup	sugar
3 tbsp	honey
1/3 cup	candied orange peel, finely chopped
1/2 tsp	cinnamon
1/2 tsp	ginger
1/4 tsp	cloves
25 seeds	cardamom, freshly crushed
1/2 tsp	baking soda
1/8 tsp	salt
2 3/4 cups	dark rye flour
1–3 tbsp	milk (optional)

Filling

1 cup	apricot or plum jam
1 cup	chopped walnuts or almonds
1 cup	raisins
1	egg yolk, for brushing the top of the cookies
	whole blanched almonds for on top of the cookies

Mix the eggs and sugar thoroughly, add the honey, then add the orange peel, spices, soda and salt. Incorporate the rye flour, adding a little milk if necessary. Divide the dough in two and refrigerate it for four hours. Roll out one part and press thinly onto a buttered cookie sheet (11 x 17 inches). Spread with all the jam and sprinkle with all the nuts and raisins.

Roll out the second half of the dough and place it on top of the filling, then press it down firmly. (This is important; otherwise, the cookies will fall apart after they are baked.)

Let the Lebkuchen rest overnight.

Preheat the oven to 300°F. Cut into oblongs, brush the top with beaten egg yolk, and press one or more whole blanched almonds into each cookie.

Bake at 300°F for 25 minutes, until golden; re-cut while hot. Cool and store in a tin.

Note: This recipe is very forgiving and has been good even if I have forgotten the nuts or the raisins. I usually make Lebkuchen at Christmas and store the rye flour in the freezer between seasons.

German Jam Cakes

Svetlana Borshevsky

I was first given this bar during spring break in North Bay, Ontario, by a fellow University College resident, Joanne Vaughan. I requested her mom's recipe, but Joanne was not forthcoming with it. She left me no alternative but to resort to kidnapping Bartholomew, her lime-green, broken-necked stuffed dragon. The recipe was soon placed in my hot little paws.

I left to go to Queen's University in Kingston the next year, taking the recipe with me. The bars disappeared fast and furiously among my fellow hobbits at Elrond College Co-op, especially when they had previously indulged in the aromatic "tobacco" that wafted through the halls in those days. After graduation I left Kingston for Toronto and accidentally left my cookbooks behind. A friend offered to send them to me, but somehow they were lost in the bowels of Canada Post.

For many years, I languished German-Jam-Cakes-less—until I remembered that I had once given the recipe to my mother. After months of my nagging, she searched through her recipe collection and found it. Now the recipe is written on the inside cover of a cookies-and-bars book I have, and it will rest there until I go to that great kitchen in the sky.

Makes 3 to 4 dozen cakes

6 cups	flour
4 cups	sugar
4 tsp	baking powder
1–2 tsp	nutmeg
4 tsp	cinnamon
3	eggs
4 tsp	vanilla
1 tsp	almond extract
2 cups	whole blanched almonds, coarsely chopped
1 lb	margarine (not butter—it just doesn't taste the same)
2 cups	dark plum jam (preferably homemade)

Now comes the time for all good cooks to become atavistic. Throw all of the above, except the jam, higgledy-piggledy into a honking huge bowl. I suppose you can mix it with a spoon but hands work a lot better—and are a lot more fun! Shmush it all together until it is well mixed and has the consistency of pie-crust dough. (CBC baker's note: We used a pastry blender to initially cut the margarine into the mixture, then finished up by using our hands. It took about half an hour to thoroughly mix everything, so don't get discouraged.)

Preheat your oven to 400°F.

Wrangle the dough into a jelly-roll pan (11 x 17 x $^3/_4$ inches). (CBC baker's note: There is a lot of dough, so you really need the big pan.) Press and smooth the mixture firmly into the pan, until it is approximately $^1/_2$ inch thick. I use a wee little antique wooden rolling pin, which fits perfectly, to smooth the mixture down. Leaving a 1-inch border around the outside jam-free, smear a skiff coat of jam on top of the mixture. (CBC baker's note: If you spread the jam right up to the edges, it could easily burn around the outside—we found out the hard way!)

Bake at 400°F for 20 to 25 minutes but keep an eye on it—the crust should be golden brown and the jam should be set, no longer runny. Cool in the pan, then cut into squares.

Fruit and Nut Crescents

Lois Klassen

My friend Maggie was a Christmas maniac. By November her house was deco-rated in every corner; she even had a special Christmas shower curtain for the bathroom. Maggie moved away many years ago, but for five or six years in a row, when our children were small, Maggie's Christmas cookie exchange was the party of the year. Maybe that was because as well as doing her share of the baking, Maggie made the eggnog from scratch and, since she was from Virginia, spiked it liberally with Southern Comfort.

Party preparations started in late October. Each of Maggie's friends would choose a special cookie recipe and submit it to her in advance so that she could compile the handouts. Then each of us would make dozens of cookies using our chosen recipe: one dozen for each of the invitees and an extra dozen to bring for sampling. If you do the math, this meant that each partygoer could expect to eat at least a dozen cookies before waddling (or staggering) home with her Christmas baking.

I still have a file folder with all of the handouts from Maggie's cookie exchanges. My favourite recipe is this one, which I have adapted. I still make it every Christmas. A guest one year exclaimed, "These are the best things I have ever put in my mouth!"

Makes 64 cookies

Dough

1/2 lb	cream cheese
1/2 lb	unsalted butter
2 cups	all-purpose flour
1/2 tsp	salt
1/3 cup	cold water
1 tsp	vanilla

Filling

1/2 cup	walnuts, finely chopped
3/4 cup	golden raisins, finely chopped
1/2 cup	apricot preserves (or jam)
1 tbsp	brandy, apple schnapps, Cointreau or Grand Marnier

Cinnamon sugar

1/4 cup	sugar
1 tbsp	cinnamon

Dough: Cream the cream cheese, butter, flour and salt together with a pastry blender (as if making pie dough). Mix the cold water and vanilla and sprinkle over the dough. Mix lightly, gather into a ball, wrap in plastic wrap and refrigerate overnight.

Filling: Combine all of the filling ingredients in a bowl.

Cinnamon sugar: In separate bowl, mix the sugar and cinnamon.

To make the cookies, preheat the oven to 375°F.

Take the dough out of the refrigerator and divide it in four. Working with one quarter at a time (keeping the rest chilled), form each quarter into a ball and roll it out on a board to make a 12-inch circle. (CBC baker's note: It may help to roll out the dough between two sheets of floured waxed paper, as it is very soft and sticky.)

Sprinkle each circle with 1 tbsp of the cinnamon sugar. Cut the circle into 16 equal wedges. Place ¼–½ tsp of the fruit and nut filling at the wide end of each wedge. Roll up the wedges and shape into crescents. Place them points-down on an ungreased cookie sheet.

Bake at 375°F for 15 to 20 minutes or until golden brown (watch carefully as they burn easily).

Almond Fingers

Jo Cannon

Here follows a recipe from my family's Depression years in Ontario, remembered as a favourite with all the crowd who turned up for Sunday afternoon tea. During a visit to my sister in England in 1991, I disinterred several of our mother's recipes from a welter of family papers. This one is surprisingly lavish, with butter and eggs. But as I recall, we had a small flock of chickens—and a neighbour with a Jersey cow! After 70-plus years of oblivion, I feel this confection deserves a triumphant comeback.

Makes 3 dozen cookies

Base and topping

1 cup	semolina
1 cup	all-purpose flour
1 cup	sugar
2 tsp	baking powder
1 cup	butter
2	eggs, beaten
2 tsp	almond extract

Filling

1 cup	jam (or more, depending on your taste)

Preheat the oven to 350°F.

Base and topping: Sift together all of the dry ingredients. Rub in the butter. Add the almond extract with the beaten eggs and stir thoroughly. (The batter will be very soft.) Spoon half of the mixture into greased pan (9 x 13 inches is about right) and smooth out.

Spread the base with the jam. (Homemade, of course. Apricot is a fine choice, though raspberry or blackberry are more colourful.)

Spoon the second half of the mixture on top.

Bake at 350°F for 20 to 30 minutes, or until golden. Let cool in the pan, on a rack, then slice into fingers.

Delight Tarts

Betty Nielson

W hen I was working in the early 1970s at Sunnyhill Hospital for Children as a physiotherapist, we had many fabulous volunteers. Our department had a very special one by the name of Helen Kelly. Not only did she volunteer in the department several times a week, but on Fridays she brought us fresh-baked goodies for afternoon coffee break. This recipe was one of my favourites. I still use her hand-written copy. These always remind me of Mrs. Kelly and special times at the hospital.

Makes about 2 dozen tarts

1/2 cup	butter
3/4 cup	sugar
2	eggs, unbeaten
2 cups	sifted flour
2 tsp	baking powder
1/8 tsp	salt

Filling

1 cup	raspberry jam (black-berry or blackcurrant jam also work well)
1/2 cup	chopped nuts

Preheat the oven to 375°F.

Cream together the butter and sugar. Add the eggs and mix well. Sift together the flour, baking powder and salt. Combine the wet and dry mixtures thoroughly.

Form the dough into small balls and press into the bottom and up the side of small (1 3/4-inch diameter) greased muffin pans. Mix together the jam and nuts and fill the centre of each tart in the muffin pans.

Bake at 375°F for 12 to 15 minutes, until light golden. Can be iced with butter icing and sprinkled with finely chopped nuts when cool.

Cranberry Tassies

Janet Renfroe

Thirty-three years ago, my husband and I lived on Hornby Island, a small gem of an island off the east coast of Vancouver Island. With the help of an elderly neighbour, Mrs. Bond, I made these Cranberry Tassies for our first Christmas there. They have been a "must bake" every Christmas since. Since these cookies are such a hit with my family, I usually triple the cookie base, but there is still about a cup of conserve left over. Spoon it over ice cream or serve it with the turkey.

Makes about 2 dozen cookies

Cookie dough

3 oz	cream cheese
1/2 cup	butter
1 cup	flour, sifted

Cranberry conserve

3 cups	raw cranberries
1	orange, peeled and chopped
1	red apple, chopped (not peeled)
2 cups	sugar
1/3 cup	Grand Marnier
1/2 cup	pecans, chopped

Cookie dough: Combine the cream cheese, butter and flour thoroughly. Divide the dough in two and chill in the refrigerator.

Conserve: Simmer all of the conserve ingredients except the Grand Marnier and pecans until tender. Remove from the heat, add the Grand Marnier and pecans, and cool.

To make the cookies, preheat the oven to 350°F.

Roll out the cookie base, half at a time, 1/4 inch thick. Cut with a small round cookie cutter and place the cookies on an ungreased cookie sheet. Place 1 tsp of the cooled cranberry conserve on each cookie (drain excess liquid when placing the conserve on the cookies so each 1 tsp is mostly fruit and nuts). Bake at 350°F for 20 minutes.

Best-Ever Fruit Bars

Verna Macdonald

My husband loves Matrimonial Bars. One day, to please him, I started to prepare a batch, but I found that I was woefully short of dates (the traditional ingredient). I did, however, have lots of prunes and dried apricots. Voila: our now-favourite recipe for bars! The original recipe was based on one found in an old Purity Flour cookbook dating back to the 1950s.

Makes 16 to 20 bars

Filling

1 cup	pitted and chopped dates
1/2 cup	pitted and chopped prunes
1/2 cup	pitted and chopped dried apricots
3/4 cup	water
	juice of 1 lemon
2 tbsp	brown sugar

Crumb mixture

1 cup	all-purpose flour
1/2 tsp	baking powder
1/8 tsp	salt
1 cup	butter or margarine (or 1/2 cup if you're being good!)
1 cup	brown sugar, lightly packed
2 cups	rolled oats

Filling: Put all of the filling ingredients in a saucepan and bring to a boil. Cook for about 5 minutes or until the dates are soft and can be mashed with a fork. (Keep an eye on the mixture, stirring often so it doesn't stick and burn.) The mixture should have the consistency of jam. Set aside and cool.

Crumb mixture: Sift together the flour, baking powder and salt. Cut in the butter or margarine with two knives or a pastry blender. Blend together until it looks crumbly. Then blend in the brown sugar and rolled oats and mix thoroughly.

Preheat the oven to 325°F.

Spread half of the crumb mixture over the bottom of a greased 9-inch square baking pan, and pat it down to make the base. Cover evenly with the cooled fruit mixture. Then cover the fruit mixture with the remaining crumb mixture, patting it down until the top is smooth. Bake at 325°F for 35 to 40 minutes or until a light golden brown. Cool before cutting into squares.

Blackberry Surprise Cookies

Alan Sirulnikoff

I can't say the early versions of this recipe were a complete success, let alone a favourite, among hiking companions and others who sampled them, but things have changed. A few summers back, in the midst of picking blackberries, I at last came up with a name for my invention: Blackberry Surprise Cookies. The surprise comes on a few levels: the variable ingredients, the tastiness of these weighty and odd-looking creatures and, of late, the surprise of those who had only tried earlier versions.

Makes 18 to 20 cookies

¹/₂ cup	flax seeds
	boiling water
¹/₄ cup	apple cider vinegar
2 or 3	ripe bananas, mashed
³/₄ cup	blackberries or applesauce
¹/₄ cup	oil (sesame mixed with olive oil is best)
¹/₄–¹/₂ cup	nut butter
¹/₂ cup	honey or maple syrup
¹/₄ cup	brown sugar (or ¹/₃ tsp stevia)
1 cup	rolled oats (not quick-cooking)
1 cup	whole wheat flour
³/₄ cup	cornmeal flour
¹/₂ cup	buckwheat or spelt flour
³/₄ cup	unsweetened coconut
¹/₂–³/₄ tsp	baking powder
¹/₂–³/₄ tsp	non-aluminum baking soda
1 tsp	cinnamon
¹/₂ tsp	salt
¹/₄ cup	sesame seeds
¹/₂–³/₄ cup	chocolate chips

Preheat the oven to 350°F.

Pour just enough boiling water over the flax seeds to more than cover them, enough to allow for expansion. After about 5 minutes, whip this with a fork (the mixture works similarly to eggs). Puree the flax with the apple cider vinegar, bananas, berries, oil, nut butter, honey and sugar, then add the oats to this mixture.

Mix the flours and all other dry ingredients, including the sesame seeds and chocolate chips.

Add the dry ingredients to the moist ones and mix completely.

A small ice cream scoop is very helpful here. Scoop up some mix, plop it onto a lightly buttered cookie sheet and lightly press it down with a fork or fingertip. Bake at 350°F for about 15 to 20 minutes or until the bottom is lightly browned and the top is firm to the touch.

Note: For optimum eating pleasure, use organic ingredients and Belgian chocolate chips.

Cherry Flips

Michelle Loroff

This recipe goes back as far as I can remember. Cherry Flips: these cookies evoke memories of Christmas past, when I could hardly wait to have the first one, followed by many others. Mom made these every Christmas, and that was the only time of year we had these tasty morsels in our home. They are not only delicious but very pretty, like cookies made for a princess.

Makes 36 to 40 cookies

1 cup	butter
1/2 cup	icing sugar
2	egg yolks
1 tsp	almond extract
2 cups	white flour
1/4 tsp	salt
1 jar	red maraschino cherries (250 mL), drained, syrup reserved

Icing

2 cups	icing sugar
	cherry syrup
	cream
1 cup	crushed walnuts

Cream the butter and 1/2 cup icing sugar; add the egg yolks and almond extract. Beat well. Mix in the flour and salt a small amount at a time, until a dough forms. Chill.

Preheat the oven to 325°F.

Work with small amount of dough at a time, keeping the rest chilled. For each cookie, take a cherry-sized piece of dough and flatten it in your palm, then fold it around a maraschino cherry. Use just enough dough to cover the cherry. Do not overwork. Place cookies on a greased cookie sheet and bake at 325°F for approximately 20 to 25 minutes. Cool.

Cherry pink icing: Use approximately 2 cups of icing sugar, and add the cherry syrup and cream by feel. You may need more sugar, depending on how much liquid you use. The icing should not be too thin, or it will just run off of your cookies.

Ice each cooled cookie and dip it into the crushed walnuts. Enjoy!

Lemon Squares by Mona Brun

Sheila Peacock

This recipe is in a publication called Cooking with Mona, which was first printed in September 1977. Mona Brun was the Food Consultant for Woodward's Food Floors, part of the Woodward's department stores in Western Canada. She appeared on many TV food programs throughout the West, and this book contains the most popular recipes tested and developed by Mona and the staff during her fourteen-year association with Woodward's. For many people who grew up in Vancouver, Woodward's Food Floors were the place to shop until 1992, when, sadly, all Woodward's stores closed their doors.

The reason my mother, Donna, gave this recipe to me to launch our Squares & Bars Recipe Contest on CBC Radio is because it's nearly identical to the lemon squares recipe her mother, Grace, used to make back in the 1930s. Donna grew up on a farm, first in Lethbridge, Alberta, and then in Creston, B.C. She remembers this as a special recipe because although they had lots of butter, milk and eggs, lemons were a real treat on the Prairies in the winter, especially in the thirties, when there was no money for extravagance. She believes Grace originally got the recipe from the Winnipeg Free Press, and although she couldn't find Grace's original scrap of paper, she does remember that my grandmother had written on it "Stays fresh for one week in the dumbwaiter"! In tribute to Donna Peacock, Grace Mulligan and Mona Brun, three ladies who understand that a true treat counts no calories, here's a delicious recipe for lemon squares.

Makes 18 to 24 squares

Base

2 cups	flour (lightly spooned into the measuring cup)
1/2 cup	icing sugar
1 cup	butter, softened

Filling

4	eggs
2 cups	sugar
6 tbsp	fresh lemon juice
1 tsp	grated lemon zest
1/4 cup	flour
1/4 tsp	baking powder
1/4 tsp	salt
	sifted icing sugar for topping

Preheat the oven to 350°F.

Base: Using a pastry blender or two knives, mix all the flour, icing sugar and butter together until the mixture resembles crumbs, then press it into the bottom of a greased pan 9 x 13 inches. Bake at 350°F for 20 minutes.

Filling: While the base is in the oven, beat the eggs slightly, then add the sugar, lemon juice and lemon zest. Sift together the flour, baking powder and salt. Add the flour mixture to the egg-lemon mixture and beat only until smooth. Pour the filling over the baked base as soon as it is removed from the oven. Return the pan to the oven and continue baking at 350°F for approximately 25 minutes or until done.

Sift extra icing sugar over top while cake is still warm (not hot). (For a decorative touch, place a paper doily with open design on the square. Sprinkle with sifted icing sugar, lift doily straight up to remove, and the design will remain on the square.) Cut into squares when cool.

"Lemon Bars" was originally published by Woodward's in 1977, in *Cooking with Mona*. Whitecap Books is republishing this consummate cookbook in Spring 2003 as part of their Canadian Classic Cookbooks series.

Mazurek

Marilyn Archibald

*T*his recipe is copied from a yellowed sheet of paper handwritten by my mother. She made these squares only at Christmas, and as I prepare to bake them, I am transported back in time to snowy Winnipeg and the gathering of all my cousins, aunts and uncles on our traditional Polish Christmas Eve.

One Christmas Eve, just before midnight, as we piled into the '57 Pontiac, we looked in utter astonishment—adults and children alike—to see none other than Santa Claus going from house to house on my grandmother's snow-covered street. The drive home was one of awe and anticipation. When we came to our house—yes, he had been there, too!

Makes approximately
4 dozen squares

Base

1/2 cup	butter, softened
3/4 cup	sugar
1	egg, beaten
2 cups	flour, sifted
1/4 tsp	salt
3–4 tbsp	milk

Topping

1 cup	raisins
1 cup	chopped dates
1 cup	chopped nuts
1/2 cup	sugar
2	eggs, beaten
2 tbsp	lemon juice
	juice and grated zest of 1 orange
1/2 cup	chopped red and green glacé cherries
1/2 cup	sliced almonds

Preheat the oven to 350°F.

Base: Cream together the butter, sugar and egg. Sift together the flour and salt. Stir the flour mixture into the butter mixture alternately with enough milk to form a stiff dough. Pat the dough evenly into a greased jelly-roll pan 10 x 15 inches. Bake at 350°F for 20 to 25 minutes, until the edges are lightly coloured.

Topping: Mix the raisins, chopped dates, chopped nuts, sugar, eggs, lemon juice, orange juice and orange zest together and spread over the baked layer hot out of the oven. Put the pan back into the oven and continue baking for about 20 minutes. Keep checking it and remove it from the oven when crust is golden brown.

While the squares are hot, decorate them with the chopped cherries and sliced almonds. Cool and cut into 1 1/2-inch squares.

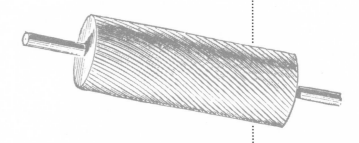

Nut and Peanut Butter Cookies, Bars and Squares

Vivian Fitzell Heron's Peanut Whirligig Cookies

Colleen Ireland

I was very lucky to have a stay-at-home mother while I grew up in the 1950s and 1960s. One reason was my mother's cooking and baking. She seemed to spend hours and hours in the kitchen whipping up delicious dishes and scrumptious baked goodies. I still have fond memories of grilled cheese and bacon sandwiches served with tomato soup when we came home from school for lunch. For dessert she might serve made-from-scratch Napoleans or a Boston cream pie. For my birthday, I always got a cake beautifully decorated with Mom's not-too-sweet icing to look like a wicker basket overflowing with flowers.

Mom's firm and crunchy chocolate chip cookies, her soft and chewy fig newtons and her oatmeal cookies are all delightful, but in recent years, she tells me, one special cookie has become the all-time favourite among the members of her choir. My mom has belonged to the choral society in Courtenay, B.C., for almost twenty years and is one of the remaining founding members. As well as being a wonderful soprano (she grew up singing in her church choir in Winnipeg), she is the society's librarian and resident cookie maker. Having tested countless recipes on her fellow choir members over the years, she says this one tops the list. I've tasted the recipe and can attest to its melt-in-your-mouth goodness.

Makes approximately 18 cookies

1/2 cup	shortening
1/2 cup	white sugar
1/2 cup	brown sugar
1/2 cup	peanut butter
1	egg, beaten
1 tsp	vanilla
1/2 tsp	baking soda
1 1/4 cups	flour
1/2 tsp	salt
3/4 cup	chocolate pieces, melted

Cream the shortening, sugars and peanut butter. Add the egg and vanilla and mix well. Mix the dry ingredients together and add them to the creamed ones. Roll out the dough on waxed paper to a thickness of about 1/4 inch. Spread the melted chocolate over the dough, then roll up the dough jelly-roll style. Chill for 15 to 30 minutes (just until the chocolate sets).

Preheat the oven to 375°F. Cut the chilled roll of dough into 1/4-inch slices. Place the slices on a greased cookie sheet and bake at 375°F for 12 minutes.

Butter Pecan Crescents

Jean Wightman

This recipe is one of my favourites. It always turn out well. As the cookies bake, the kitchen is filled with the most delightful aroma. These cookies also freeze well. They are delicious and make wonderful gifts.

Makes approximately 3 dozen cookies

2 cups	all-purpose flour
1/4 tsp	salt
1/4 cup	cornstarch
1/3 cup	butter (not margarine), softened
1 cup	sifted icing sugar
2 tsp	grated lemon zest
3/4 cup	finely chopped pecans icing sugar to sprinkle on cookies

Preheat the oven to 325°F.

Sift together the flour and salt. Mix in the cornstarch. In a large bowl, cream the butter, then gradually blend in the icing sugar. Add the dry ingredients to the creamed mixture a little at a time, combining well after each addition. Add and mix in the lemon zest and pecans.

Using 1 tsp of dough for each cookie, shape the dough in your hands to form crescents. Place the crescents on ungreased cookie sheets and bake at 325°F for 12 to 15 minutes. (Note: If you make the crescent shapes bigger, they will need extra time in the oven. Try not to have the middle part of the crescents too fat.)

While the crescents are still warm, sprinkle them lightly with sifted icing sugar.

Buckeyes

Jennifer Zuk

When I was a young girl, my mother made luscious peanut-butter balls that would melt in your mouth. I just loved them! Alas, when I asked her for the recipe several years after moving out of the house, Mom told me she had lost it. Luckily, twenty years ago I met my good friend Moe. Her sister-in-law in Ohio would send her some of these Buckeyes every year from the batches she made with her church auxiliary ladies' group. When I tasted them, I knew I had found the elusive peanut-butter ball recipe. These are even better than my mother's, because they are decadently dipped in chocolate.

Makes 200 to 250 cookies

1 lb	butter
2 lbs	peanut butter
3 lbs	icing sugar

Coating

2–3 lbs	semi-sweet or baker's chocolate, melted

Combine the butter, peanut butter and icing sugar in a large bowl and mix well, kneading to blend in all of the icing sugar.

Roll the dough into 1-inch balls, and shape these into ovals. Place on cookie sheets covered with waxed paper and insert a toothpick into the centre of each oval. Put the cookie sheets in the freezer for 5 to 10 minutes.

While the cookies are hardening in the freezer, melt the chocolate in a bowl.

Remove the cookie sheets from the freezer and dip each peanut-butter oval into the chocolate, coating the sides but leaving the top bare. Place the dipped balls back on the waxed paper, remove the toothpicks and smooth over the holes with the back of a spoon. After the chocolate has set, store the Buckeyes in an airtight container in the refrigerator.

Note: You can easily adjust the quantity of this recipe. Just remember the ratio of 1:2:3 by weight of butter, peanut butter and icing sugar. For example, a small batch would take 1/4 lb butter, 1/2 lb peanut butter and 3/4 lb icing sugar. The amount of melted chocolate that's needed can vary, depending on who's doing the dipping and how big a batch you make. If you buy 3 lbs for the full recipe, it will be plenty and you can always find something to do with the leftover chocolate.

Marie's Treats

Jill Scott

I call these "Marie's Treats" because my friend's mom, Marie (God rest her soul), gave me this recipe years ago. When she made them for me she would pretend they were very difficult, but once she gave in and sent me the recipe, I found out how incredibly easy they are.

No matter who you serve these to, they always disappear, and someone always asks for the recipe. The trick to maximizing their tastiness is to serve them straight from the freezer. Storing them in the freezer also means the kids don't know they are there, so you have a secret stash for private nibbling.

Makes 2 dozen cookies

	graham wafers (whole)
1 cup	butter
1 cup	brown sugar
1 cup	sliced almonds

Line a pan 9 x 13 inches with foil, shiny side down, and cover the bottom with one layer of graham wafers.

Preheat the oven to 350°F.

Bring the butter and sugar to a boil, then add the almonds and mix well. Spread over the graham wafers.

Bake at 350°F for 6 to 8 minutes; watch carefully, as it burns easily. Put in the freezer and slice when frozen (the squares will be very crumbly).

Rocky Road Squares

Kathryn Marlow

Five years ago, when I was sixteen, I discovered that I had a gluten allergy. All of a sudden, I had to give up bread, bagels, pizza, pasta, cake, cookies...you get the point! For someone who was never a big fan of rice, a future of rice, rice cakes, rice crackers, etc., looked pretty dismal. There were recipes for gluten-free food of all sorts, but they called for elaborate combinations of rice flour, chick pea flour, xanthan gum, and so on. (Did I mention that I hate cooking?) Eventually, out of desperation for sweets, I began to experiment with various combinations of Rice Krispies, chocolate chips, peanut butter, corn syrup and marshmallows.

One day, I discovered a recipe on the back of a corn syrup bottle. This was the recipe for Rocky Road Squares. They were easy, no-bake, more interesting than what I had been making—and good! My brother and I polished off the first pan in a day or two. The next time I went to a friend's house, I made some to take with me, and they were a definite hit. They're very chocolatey and rich, but oh so yummy. I've added them to my gluten-free, no-bake squares cache, and I always take them to group events and on camping trips.

Makes approximately 20 squares

1/2 cup	corn syrup
1 cup	chocolate chips
1/2 cup	peanut butter
3 cups	miniature marshmallows
2 1/2 cups	Rice Krispies cereal

Heat the corn syrup and chocolate chips until the chocolate chips have melted. Add the peanut butter. In a separate bowl, mix the marshmallows and cereal. Add the cereal mixture to the peanut butter mixture. Press into a buttered 9-inch square pan and refrigerate.

Nanny's Peanut Butter Cookies

Sarah Rocchi

My grandmother, Nanny, used to make these cookies for us when we were children. Now that we've grown up, and the grandkids are scattered across North America (from Prince George to California), the only time we get to visit Nanny is when we come home for Christmas. Nanny always makes a batch of these sand-coloured, melt-in-your-mouth cookies for our visits. They may not be the flashiest cookies on the tray of sweets, but they're always the first ones gone.

Makes 6 dozen cookies

1 cup	shortening
1 cup	white sugar
1 cup	brown sugar
1 cup	smooth peanut butter
2	eggs
2 cups	cake and pastry flour
2 tsp	baking soda
1/4 tsp	salt

Preheat the oven to 375°F.

Cream together the shortening and sugars. Add the peanut butter and beat well. Add the eggs and beat them in. In a separate bowl, mix together the flour, baking soda and salt. Add the dry ingredients gradually to the peanut butter mixture, mixing until everything is well combined.

Drop by teaspoonfuls onto an ungreased cookie sheet. Press down with a fork. Bake at 375°F for 12 to 15 minutes.

Healthy Rice Krispies Squares

Hannah Galloway

This recipe was given to me three-and-a-half years ago, when I found out that my five-year-old daughter, Zoe, is an insulin-dependent diabetic. I was devastated by the diagnosis and worried, as any mother would, about how this new life structured around meal plans and no treats was going to affect my daughter's joie de vivre.

This is a fabulous, gluten-free, low-sugar treat that is high in protein. Best of all, these squares are really good!

Makes 1 dozen generous squares

1/2 cup	peanut butter (or 1/4 cup almond butter and 1/4 cup tahini)
1/2 cup	honey (or rice syrup)
1 tsp	vanilla
1/4 tsp	salt
2 cups	Rice Krispies cereal

Combine the peanut butter (or almond butter and tahini) and honey (or rice syrup) in a saucepan and heat until softened. Remove from the heat and stir in the vanilla and salt. Mix in the cereal. Flatten the mixture in an oiled 8-inch square pan. Chill 1 to 2 hours before cutting into squares.

Bees' Knees Squares

Suzie Sims

O n a trip into the Purcell Wilderness Conservancy one summer, the food was organized by Jennifer Wolfe of Mayerthorpe, Alberta. I dubbed Jennifer the "Martha Stewart of the Back Country" for the way she used her own home-ground cereal grains and organic ingredients, providing healthier meals than many such trips offer. Since there was a restriction on the weight our pack mules could carry, Jennifer's meals and goodies were compact, required virtually no cooking (cutting down on fuel requirements) and were highly nutritious.

The five participants and our guide/wrangler hiked all day, joining the pack-string for lunch and at the chosen campsite at the end of each day. Over the fourteen days we climbed 10,544 ft. and dropped way back down, gaining a mere 100 ft. overall. Given the less-than-ideal weather conditions, Jennifer's meals were a most welcome aspect of this spectacularly scenic trip. The following is my favourite of the various cookies and squares Jennifer made for us.

Makes 2 dozen squares

1 cup	butter, softened
1/3 cup	honey
1 tsp	vanilla
1 1/2 cups	quick-cooking rolled oats
1 1/2 cups	unbleached white flour
1 cup	butterscotch chips
2 tbsp	honey
1/2 cup	slivered almonds

Preheat the oven to 375°F.

Beat the butter in a bowl, then add 1/3 cup honey and the vanilla, mixing until smooth. Stir in the oats, flour and butterscotch chips. Spread the mixture in a greased baking pan 9 x 13 inches. Heat the 2 tbsp honey until it's runny and dab or brush it onto the surface of the dough. Sprinkle the slivered almonds on top, then push them down into the dough.

Bake at 375°F for about 25 minutes or until golden brown.

Cool a little before cutting; once thoroughly cooled, cut into final squares to fit in a milk carton. Seal in plastic individually (vacuum seal if possible); put the wrapped squares into the milk carton and seal it with masking tape. Can be labelled and frozen, if desired.

Gooey Squares

Jennifer Abrams

Although this family recipe is not an oldie, it will forever be described as a goodie. I went home for a family visit and, as usual, I did not get in until very late. It's amazing, but it does not matter how long I've been away from home, as soon as I cross the threshold my first stop is always the kitchen. It can be two or three in the morning, but it does not matter. Dad, Ely and I will sit at the table, El will have a tea, Dad, a Perrier and I'll always have a nosh…I am not entirely convinced that I even need to be hungry for this ritual!

Makes 30 squares

Base

1 cup	*flour*
¼ cup	*sugar*
⅓ cup	*butter or margarine, softened*

Topping

2	*eggs*
½ cup	*sugar*
½ cup	*corn syrup*
2 tbsp	*butter or margarine, melted*
1 cup	*chocolate chips*
¾ cup	*raw walnuts or pecans, coarsely chopped*

Preheat the oven to 350°F.

Base: Combine the flour, sugar and butter or margarine, mixing until crumbly. Press firmly into a greased 9-inch square pan. Bake at 350°F for 12 to 15 minutes or until light brown.

Topping: Beat the eggs, sugar, corn syrup and butter or margarine until blended. Stir in the chocolate chips and nuts. Pour the topping evenly over the base and bake at 350°F for 25 to 30 minutes or until set and golden.

Cool, then cut into squares.

Barb's Peanut Butter Squares

Barb Wallington

This recipe is a combination of two other recipes. One day, I set out to make my standard chocolate-chip oatmeal cookies, but then I remembered I had some peanut butter filling in the fridge left over from making peanut butter cups. These squares are what I ended up with. When my husband tried them, he said they were so good that I had to enter them in a contest. So I did! (CBC baker's note: The peanut butter layer is the pièce de résistance in this recipe!)

Makes 18 to 24 squares

Oatmeal cookie mixture

1 cup	margarine or butter, softened
1 1/4 cups	brown sugar, firmly packed
1/2 cup	granulated sugar
2	eggs
2 tbsp	milk
2 tsp	vanilla
1 3/4 cups	all-purpose flour
2 1/2 cups	rolled oats
1 tsp	baking soda
1/2 tsp	salt (optional)

Peanut butter layer

1/4 cup	brown sugar
1/2 cup	icing sugar
1/2 tsp	vanilla
2 tbsp	butter, softened
3/4 cup	smooth peanut butter

Chocolate layer

2 cups	semi-sweet chocolate chips (can substitute carob chips)

Preheat the oven to 350°F.

Oatmeal cookie mixture: Beat the margarine or butter with sugars until creamy. Add the eggs, milk and vanilla and beat well. In a separate bowl, stir together the flour, oats, baking soda and salt. Add the flour mixture to the butter mixture until blended (no need to overmix).

Crumble half of the cookie mixture into a greased glass baking dish 9 x 13 inches. Lightly press the mixture to spread it evenly, then pat it down.

Peanut butter layer: Mix together all of the ingredients for the peanut butter layer until well blended. Drop all of this mixture by spoonfuls on top of the cookie layer, spreading it evenly. This is a very sticky process! Lightly press the peanut butter mixture into place by hand—you will need to wet your hands to keep the mixture from sticking to you, but a little water won't hurt the bar!

Chocolate layer: Spread the chocolate chips evenly over the peanut butter layer.

Finish by crumbling the remaining half of the cookie mixture over the chocolate layer and gently pressing it into place. You will probably need to wet your hands for this layer, too!

Bake at 350°F for approximately 20 to 25 minutes, depending on your oven and the level of chewiness you prefer. Cool, then cut into squares. Lift them out of the pan with a metal spatula.

Almond Pretzels

Moira Wightman

These cookies have been a family favourite for many years. It is not just the eating that has become a tradition, but the making and shaping, with some odd shapes appearing on the cookie sheet. The recipe came from a cookbook that was an engagement present from an English friend. I had been born and brought up in South Africa and was about to marry a Canadian. The book was from the United States and was possibly the only North American cookbook available in the U.K. in 1965.

Makes 3 to 4 dozen cookies

1 cup	butter
1 cup	sugar
2	egg yolks
2	whole eggs
1/2 lb	ground almonds
2 cups	flour

Cream the butter and sugar, then add the egg yolks and whole eggs. Mix in the almonds (unblanched) and flour, knead well, and shape into a large roll. Chill in the refrigerator. (CBC baker's note: Chill for at least 2 hours.)

Preheat the oven to 325°F.

Cut the chilled dough into pieces the size of walnuts. In the palm of your hands, roll the pieces into ropes 1/2 inch in diameter and form into pretzels, rings, hearts, crescents or other shapes. Place the cookies on a greased cookie sheet and bake at 325°F for 20 minutes.

Dory Bars

Nicky Haigh

*O*ne summer I had a craving for a granola bar. Everything at the store was either dry and crunchy or full of preservatives, and I wanted a nutritious but delicious snack. I looked through all the recipe books I could lay my hands on—at the library, friends' houses, bookstores—for a bar with fruit and nuts and not too much filler. No luck. So there was nothing for it but to develop my own recipe.

It took a few tries, but eventually everything held together. They acquired their name when I went to visit my sister on Saltspring Island. We took some bars down to the beach with us, and as we drifted around in her dory, my other sister swimming beside us, we all snacked happily. The bars and the dory were an ideal combination. After each chunk of bar, we'd trail our hands over the side to wash off the stickiness. The bars developed past the sticky stage, but the name stuck.

Makes approximately 70 bars

Dry ingredients

3 cups	Crispy rice cereal (like Rice Krispies)
2 1/2 cups	almonds, chopped
1/2 cup	toasted cashews
1/3 cup	pumpkin seeds
1/4 cup	toasted sesame seeds
1/2 cup	dried cranberries
1 cup	dried apricots, chopped

Syrup

1/2 cup	sugar
1/2 cup	real maple syrup
1/2 cup	honey

Combine all of the dry ingredients.

Syrup: In a large heavy saucepan, stir together the sugar, maple syrup and honey. Heat over low to medium heat until the sugar melts. Increase the heat and bring the syrup to a boil. Boil for 5 minutes, then turn off the heat.

Add the dry ingredients to the syrup and mix quickly, until just combined. Dump out into two oiled pans 8 x 10 inches. Press the mixture into the pans. (This is best done using a piece of oiled waxed paper.) Allow to set, then cut into bars.

Note: Any combination of dried fruit and nuts can be used, but these ingredients should total 5 to 5 1/2 cups.

Shortbread

Mum's Shortbread

Naida Hobbs

My mum always makes this shortbread. Though different, it is the "real" one to me. You roll these out in a ball, then flatten them. My mum uses her first two or three fingers to do that, so they are really "made by hand," and they look like you're getting a bit of her with each one. Sometimes now I make them nickel-sized and flatten them with a fork—they are just the right size to dip into the chocolate fondue. There was a bleak time in the 1970s when my holistic mum tried making these with whole wheat flour, but don't try this—it caused anarchy at our house!

Makes about 6 dozen cookies

1 lb	butter, softened
1 cup	brown sugar, packed
4 cups	flour

Preheat the oven to 300°F.

Cream the butter and sugar, then add the flour and knead well for about 10 minutes. Make into cookies (roll into balls and flatten).

Bake at 300°F for 20 minutes.

Veda's Shortbread

Karen Crispin May

When I started to work as a nurse twenty years ago, in Hamilton, Ontario, one of the older nurses on our unit brought this shortbread to our staff's Christmas party. Veda was near retirement at the time, and she was a much-loved member of our team. She imparted wisdom, experience and caring to the patients and staff of our maternity unit. Her shortbread was so different and delicious that I asked for her recipe. I make it every year, and it always gets rave reviews. I still don't think mine is quite as good as Veda's was, though.

Sadly, Veda passed away from cancer only a few years after she retired. I have many fond memories of her and am thankful for the laughs and lessons we shared. Each year when I make my shortbread, I think of her and often shed a little tear.

Makes an 8-inch square pan of shortbread

1/2 cup	brown sugar
1 cup	butter
2 cups	graham or whole wheat flour (I prefer graham)
1/8 tsp	salt

Preheat the oven to 325°F.

Cream the brown sugar and butter together, then add the flour and salt. Press into a greased 8-inch square baking pan. Cut into squares and pierce each square once or twice with a fork before baking.

Bake at 325°F for 20 to 25 minutes. Take out when the edges are just beginning to brown.

Cran-Apple White Chocolate Shortbread Bars

Katie Kelly

When I first heard of the CBC's contest, I racked my brain for an appropriate recipe—something steeped in family tradition and historical relevance. To my alarm, I realized that no traditional dessert bar recipe existed in my family. This glaring omission would have to be rectified immediately, for the sake of future generations. So I set out to make something brand new.

I wanted to use cranberries because winter is their season, apples because we had hundreds from our stalwart apple tree, and white chocolate because...well, because I love white chocolate. Armed with a delectable shortbread crust, I began a series of experiments. Many batches were baked, and I enlisted everyone within reach to provide feedback. At last my dessert was finished, and I hope this recipe will become a tradition for my family and me.

These bars are best when made with organic ingredients. And when you're looking for white chocolate, try a chocolatier's bulk supply. Those chunks of creamy heaven are much tastier than ordinary baking chocolate.

Makes 18 bars

Base

1 cup	butter, softened
1/2 cup	cane sugar
3 cups	unbleached white flour (or half white, half whole wheat pastry flour)

Filling

3 medium	apples (or 2 large)
4 cups	cranberries, fresh or frozen
1 1/4 cups	orange juice
1/2 tsp	cinnamon
1/4 tsp	cloves
1 cup	walnut pieces
1/2 lb	white chocolate (or a 225-g package of white chocolate chips)

Topping

1/8–1/4 lb	white chocolate (or 2–4 squares), to taste

Preheat the oven to 300°F.

Base: Cream the butter with an electric mixer. Add the sugar and mix well. Add the flour in four or five parts—you may have to mix by hand for the last one or two additions. Press into a greased pan 9 x 13 inches. Bake at 300°F for 10 minutes. Remove from the oven and turn up the temperature to 350°F.

Filling: While the base is in the oven, chop the apples into little pieces, peeling if desired. Place the apples in a deep pot along with the cranberries, orange juice and spices. Bring to a boil, then turn down the heat slightly, boiling gently until the cranberries pop and most of the liquid has evaporated. This should take about 15 minutes, and you'll need to stir it frequently near the end to make sure it doesn't burn. Stir in the walnuts and remove from the burner. While the filling is cooking, coarsely chop the 1/2 lb white chocolate.

Spoon the filling onto the shortbread base. Spread it around, then sprinkle on the white chocolate pieces. Mix gently until chocolate melts and is incorporated into the filling. Bake at 350°F for 20 to 30 minutes, until the base just starts to brown.

Topping: Once you have removed the pan from the oven, grate the 1/8 to 1/4 lb of white chocolate evenly over the surface of the filling. (You can use an ordinary cheese grater for this.)

Cut into bars while still warm. Chill before serving.

Sort of Chocolate Chip Shortbread

Megan Jameson

I have been making these chocolate chip cookies for so many years I can do it with my eyes shut. A few years ago I must have actually had my eyes shut, because I forgot to put in the eggs even though they were sitting on the counter. The resulting cookies were deemed by my two boys to be the best ever, and they have now become a standard in my cookie repertoire. My sons always delight in recounting this story of human error; I prefer to think of it as serendipity.

Makes 4 dozen cookies

1 cup	butter
2 cups	white sugar
1 tsp	vanilla
2 1/2 cups	flour
1 tsp	baking powder
1/4 tsp	salt
2 cups	chocolate chips

Preheat the oven to 350°F.

Beat the butter and sugar until fluffy, then add the vanilla. Mix together the flour, baking powder and salt, then add this mixture to the butter mixture. By hand, mix in the chocolate chips.

Using your hands, roll the dough into 1 1/2-inch balls. Press onto an ungreased cookie sheet and bake at 350°F for 10 to 12 minutes.

Yule Logs

Sherry Mitchell

Yule logs have been a Christmas tradition in my family for as long as I can remember. This recipe was given to my mother, Evelyn Mitchell, and she in turn passed it along to me. My two sons are now in their twenties, but even though I have made these cookies every year since they were born, they have never tired of them, and they are quick to remind me when it's Yule Log time again.

Makes 6 dozen cookies

1 cup	butter or margarine, softened
3/4 cup	sugar
2 tsp	vanilla
2 tsp	rum extract
1	egg, beaten
3 cups	unbleached white flour
1 tsp	nutmeg
1/2 tsp	salt

Icing

3 tbsp	butter or margarine
1/2 tsp	vanilla
1 tsp	rum extract
2 1/2 cups	icing sugar
2 tbsp	milk
	nutmeg for sprinkling

Preheat the oven to 350°F.

Cream the butter and sugar until well blended; add the flavourings and egg and beat until light and fluffy. Add the flour, nutmeg and salt and mix until a shortbread dough is formed, if necessary using your hands to completely work in the flour mixture.

Roll small batches of dough into ropes approximately 1/2 inch in diameter. Cut these ropes on the diagonal into pieces approximately 2 inches long. Bake on greased cookie sheets at 350°F for about 15 minutes. Cool on racks.

Icing: Combine the butter, vanilla and rum extract; blend in 1/2 cup of the icing sugar and beat until smooth, then add about 2 more cups of icing sugar alternately with the 2 tbsp of milk.

Ice the cooled cookies with the butter icing, using a knife or a cookie press with an icing attachment for a decorative effect. Sprinkle with nutmeg.

Melt-in-Your-Mouth Shortbread Drops

Grace Darney

*I*n the 1960s, I worked for a number of banks in Vancouver. One of the more interesting places was the Bank of Nova Scotia at Hastings and Columbia Streets, where I worked for a few months late in 1965. I served many interesting characters, but my favourite was an old coin collector. Because I was the bank's coin teller, I was an important contact for him, saving old coins whenever they turned up in my cash drawer. Every once in a while, he'd give me a silver dollar in appreciation. I occasionally wonder if any of the coins I found made him a fortune.

The old coin collector's wife was an awesome baker, sending cookies and cakes for the bank staff on a regular basis. She also willingly shared the recipes for these delectable goodies. I've made her shortbread drops every year since 1965 and have shared the recipe with family and friends from all parts of Canada, Japan, France and England.

Makes 2 dozen small cookies

1 lb	butter
1 cup	icing sugar
3 cups	flour
1/2 cup	cornstarch

Preheat the oven to 300°F to 325°F (low oven).

Using an electric beater, soften the butter, then slowly add the icing sugar, beating until the mixture has the consistency of whipped cream. Sift the flour and cornstarch together twice. Using a wooden spoon, gradually add the flour/cornstarch to the butter/icing sugar, beating until the mixture breaks apart. Drop the dough by spoonfuls onto an ungreased cookie sheet.

Bake at 300°F to 325°F for 30 to 40 minutes. Make sure you peek at the cookies often—they should not get too brown but should be a light tan shade.

You can decorate the tops with green or red glacé cherries before baking, or leave them plain.

The number of cookies you get depends on how small or large your spoonfuls are. I've always doubled or tripled the recipe because these cookies are so delicious.

Fresh Ginger Shortbread with White and Dark Chocolate Drizzles

Xerez Haffenden

I started life as a cookie-deprived child. My four siblings and I had only experienced the store-bought 1970s-style shortbreads (two per day) doled out along with a baloney sandwich in our lunch boxes. Rescue came when my grandparents moved in next door when I was eight: homemade cookies then became available daily. I was enlightened and have loved and made cookies ever since. My favourites were always the real shortbreads (read: butter fiend), but alas, they were made only at Christmas.

One of my most treasured possessions is my grandmother's cookbook, which was left to me. It is a 1940s Women's Farm Union of Alberta collection, which includes all of her recipes along with information on how to make soap and clean and cook porcupine (which I have yet to try).

This recipe is my adaptation of her shortbread—I added the zingy ginger and the chocolate. I make these every year with her in my thoughts.

Makes 3 to 4 dozen cookies

1 lb	butter
1 cup	icing sugar
1	egg yolk
1 heaping tsp	freshly grated ginger root
4 cups	flour
2 squares	white baking chocolate
2 squares	dark baking chocolate
2 tsp	butter (divided)

Cream the butter and sugar, then add the egg yolk and ginger. Add the flour and mix well. Refrigerate the batter for a half-hour to make it behave.

Preheat the oven to 325°F.

Roll out the dough and cut with a 2-inch star-shaped cookie cutter. Place the cookies on an ungreased cookie sheet (for perfect cookies, use parchment paper) and bake at 325°F for 15 minutes or until golden brown. Let cool on rack.

While the cookies are cooling, melt the white and dark chocolate separately, each with a teaspoon of butter. Drizzle a little melted white and a little melted dark chocolate over each cooled star and let set. Very beautiful, with a great zingy taste.

Karen's Orange-Cranberry Oatmeal Shortbread

John Drexel

Every year for the past twenty, I have baked cookies to give as Christmas and Hanukkah presents. As the final cookie is lovingly packaged (usually on Christmas morning), my better half lectures me on cutting back on baking to reduce my holiday stress. However, each year it is the same better half who finds one or two new recipes that we must try. And everyone has their favourites—so how do you cut back without disappointing someone? You don't. You take a vacation from your regular job, enlist the assistance of your daughter, roll up your sleeves, put on the stereo and bake 150 dozen cookies using twenty-two recipes over four days. One year I baked 220 dozen cookies, just to see how far I could push the envelope.

This recipe is for my significant other, who found the inspiration for it while practising her favourite pastime—reading.

Makes 3 to 4 dozen cookies

1/2 lb	butter, softened
2/3 cup	sugar
1/8 tsp	salt
2	large egg yolks
1 tsp	vanilla
2 1/3 cups	flour
1 cup	dried cranberries (soaked in hot water for 15 minutes, drained well and finely chopped)
3/4 cup	old-fashioned rolled oats or quick-cooking oats
1 1/2 tsp	freshly grated orange zest
1/2 cup	sugar to roll the cookies in

Preheat the oven to 350°F.

In a large bowl, using an electric mixer, beat together the butter, $^2/_3$ cup sugar and salt until light and fluffy. Beat in the egg yolks one at a time, then add the vanilla and beat until just combined. Mix in the flour.

Add the cranberries, oats and orange zest to the dough and mix until just combined.

Form the dough into $^3/_4$-inch balls and roll the balls in sugar to coat. Arrange the balls 2 inches apart on an ungreased cookie sheet.

Bake at 350°F for approximately 12 minutes or until the cookies are a pale golden colour.

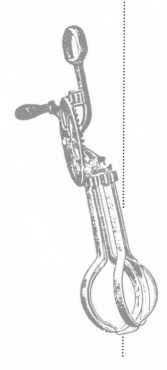

All-Round-Good Cookies,
Bars and Squares

Easy Almond Wedges

Charlene Petersen

This recipe is from my Danish-born sister-in-law, Jette Thomas. The family loved traditional Danish marzipan cakes (Kransekager), but these were expensive and time-consuming to make. This recipe duplicates the taste quite closely with a lot less work. It has become a favourite with my Canadian side of the family as well.

These wedges look quite plain and tend to be left on the dessert table until some unsuspecting soul gets tired of fancy pastries. Then they become an instant hit. At one office party, a colleague who had just eaten one ran around the room with the plate, interrupting conversations to tell people they simply had to try them. They can be made in a square cake pan, but the corners get a little overdone. You can freeze them without affecting the flavour or texture, but they usually disappear too quickly around my house to make it to the freezer.

Makes about 24 dainty or 18 larger wedges

1	egg
1 cup	white sugar
1 cup	flour
2–2 1/2 tsp	almond extract
1/2 cup	margarine, melted
	sliced almonds, for decoration (optional)

Preheat the oven to 350°F.

Beat the egg until fluffy. Add the sugar. Slowly blend in the flour, almond extract and margarine to form a thick, smooth batter. Pour into a greased 8-inch round pan, lined with waxed paper. Sprinkle with almonds, if desired.

Bake at 350°F for about 30 minutes or until lightly browned.

Famous Caramel Squares

Danielle Hopkins

I am not certain exactly when these scrumptious caramel squares became part of my life. I remember eating them with high-school friends in Ottawa and at family gatherings, but they proved their true value when I started university. My mom used to send me back to school with whatever food she could pack up frozen, to provide my friends and me with relief from the cafeteria food. During late nights of studying or gabbing, we'd unwrap these nuggets and ooooh and ahhhh.

As we "grew up," I would transport these squares in my baggage for birthdays, camping trips, baby showers and, most importantly, the final candle-burning and chocolate-eating celebration when the last of us gals finally finished our degrees. These occasions have taken place in Alberta, British Columbia, Nova Scotia and Missouri. Now I live in California, and the fame of these squares continues. Requests for girls' nights, parties and work treats really mean, "Do you have any of your mom's squares?" Careful planning and regular visits from Mom mean that I can usually answer, "Yes!"

Makes 30 squares

Bottom layer

2 cups	all-purpose flour
1/4 cup	sugar
1 cup	butter

Middle layer

1 cup	brown sugar
1 cup	butter
1/4 cup	corn syrup
1 cup	sweetened condensed milk
1 tsp	vanilla

Top layer

| 1 1/2 cups | chocolate chips |

Bottom layer: Preheat the oven to 350°F. Combine all of the ingredients until crumbly. Press firmly into a greased pan 9 x 13 inches. Bake at 350°F for 25 minutes or until light golden.

Middle layer: Place all of the ingredients except the vanilla in a heavy saucepan. Heat slowly until the sugar is dissolved, then bring to a boil and boil for 7 minutes, stirring constantly. Remove from the heat, add the vanilla and beat well. The mixture should be brown and caramel-like. Spread over the baked bottom layer and let cool.

Top layer: Melt the chocolate and spread it over the cooled middle layer.

Glass Cookies

Elsbeth Wiegand

Here is my favourite cookie recipe, which I have been using since I was a teenager (I am sixty-five now). It comes from a friend of my mother's, who learned it from her mother-in-law. The original name was "Printen from Hamburg," but because the cookies don't bear any resemblance to printen (a sort of gingerbread), I renamed them Glass Cookies—they are as fragile and brittle as glass.

Makes 10 dozen cookies

2 1/2 cups	flour
1 tbsp	baking powder
1 1/2 cups	brown or turbinado sugar
1 cup less 2 tbsp	unsalted margarine or butter
2	eggs
3/4 cup	sliced almonds

Mix the flour and baking powder. Add the sugar, then the margarine or butter and eggs. Knead into a dough. Cut the almonds into little pieces and knead them into the dough.

Form the dough into rolls about 6 inches long and about 1 1/2 to 2 inches in diameter. Wrap the rolls in waxed paper and chill them in the refrigerator overnight.

Preheat the oven to 375°F. Cut the rolls into thin slices, about 1/8 inch thick.

Place the slices on greased cookie sheets and bake at about 375°F for 5 to 6 minutes.

Vanillien Kipfeln (Vanilla Crescents)

Angelika Dawson

T he only thing I want to inherit from my mom is her cookbook: a 1963 day planner into which she has handwritten her favourite recipes, mostly in German. Baking is her ministry, and it's her Christmas cookies that friends wait most eagerly for. Mom takes a week of holidays every November and bakes mountains of them to give away. Of all the wonderful cookies she bakes, Vanillien Kipfeln are my favourite. They are firm and rich but not too sweet, perfect for dunking into a cup of coffee. The nutty smell that fills the kitchen when she bakes them is irresistible. And those lucky enough to get them at Christmas know that they are receiving a gift from the heart.

Makes 10 dozen cookies

2 cups	sugar
1 tsp	vanilla
6	large egg yolks
2 cups	butter
1 cup	ground hazelnuts or almonds (nuts must be roasted first)
1/2 tsp	baking powder
2 1/2 cups	flour
	icing sugar to roll the cookies in

Preheat the oven to 375°F.

Beat the sugar, vanilla, egg yolks and butter. Add the ground nuts. Sift the baking powder into the flour and mix into the moist ingredients to make a firm dough. To know if the dough is firm enough, take a small amount into your hand and form a crescent about the size of your pinkie. If the dough feels limp, you need to add more flour. The crescent must be firm. Shape all of the dough into crescents and place on greased cookie sheets.

Bake at 375°F until lightly golden. Let crescents cool on the cookie sheets and when still slightly warm, roll them in icing sugar.

Khrusty (pronounced *hroo-sti-ka*) or Verhuny

Christa Ovenell

This was my grandmother's recipe. We had these cookies only at Christmas and Easter. One Christmas when my grandmother was in the beginning stages of Alzheimer's, we were at my mother's house: my mom, my sister, her daughter, my grandmother and me. The full and happy kitchen was a smooth assembly line for the production of perogies and khrusty. At nineteen, I was engaged but not yet married. Suddenly my strict, eighty-nine-year-old Catholic grandmother turned to me and asked, "Are you a virgin?" Need I tell you how shocked I was? I looked to my mother for help, only to find she and my sister had fled the room to hide their laughter. Thinking quickly, I said, "Why do you want to know, Granny?" She replied, "Well, I've been thinking about this virgin birth thing." My mother had returned in time to hear this, and she put on a stern face. "Mom," she said, "what would Father Boyuchuck say to hear you talking like this?" That snapped my grandmother back to her old self, and she never again inquired about such personal matters.

I love making these cookies because they take me instantly back to that scene, and I feel the love and humour that binds a family together.

Makes 4 dozen cookies

2	whole eggs
3	egg yolks
2 tbsp	sugar
1 tbsp	rich cream
1/2 tsp	salt
1 tbsp	rum or brandy
1 cup + 2 tbsp	sifted flour
	oil for deep frying
	icing sugar

Beat the whole eggs and the yolks together until very light; add the sugar, cream, salt and rum. Stir in the flour. This dough will be very soft. Knead it on a floured board until smooth. Cover and let stand for 10 minutes.

Roll out the dough very thin ($\frac{1}{8}$ inch thick or less), using a small amount at a time and keeping the remaining dough covered so it does not dry out. With a pizza wheel or fluted pastry cutter, cut the dough into thin strips, about $1\frac{1}{4}$ inches wide. Then cut the strips into rectangles $1\frac{1}{2}$ to 2 inches long. Now, slit each rectangle in the centre lengthwise and pull one end through the slit to form a loose loop. Cover the shaped dough.

Fry a few at a time in clean, fresh deep fat (375°F) until delicately browned. Drain on racks over absorbent paper; when cool, place a few at a time in a plastic bag slightly filled with icing sugar and shake to cover.

Sue's B Squares

Sue McIntyre

I love to bake, so I decided to create my own recipe for squares. I love challenges, too, so I thought I'd try something with a theme. I was riding my bike, eating a bagel and playing the banjo when it came to me: B Squares! I set out to make a treat that uses only ingredients beginning with the letter "B." I quickly eliminated a few ingredients—bran, bulgur, bison—and picked a few that would really taste good. The result is a takeoff on the classic Blondies (Blonde Brownies).

These squares are dense and rich. The recipe makes a lot, but they freeze perfectly. Cut them small, and serve to all of your friends: Barbara, Bob, Betty, Ben... If there are any squares left over, people whose names start with other letters of the alphabet might be allowed to have some.

Makes 4 dozen squares

Base

1 cup	butter
2½ cups	brown sugar
2	brown eggs, beaten
1 cup	butterscotch chips
1 cup	blackcurrants
2 tbsp	brandy and orange liqueur (formally known as Grand Marnier, but that doesn't start with B—or substitute "banilla")
3 cups	bakers best all-purpose flour (okay, it's a stretch but how could I do it without flour?)
1 tsp	b-salt (as opposed to sea salt—b-salt comes from a box)
2 tsp	baking powder

Glaze

2 cups	B.C. Sugar Confectioners (icing) sugar
2 tbsp	brandy and orange liqueur
1–2 tbsp	best water in the world (courtesy of Super Natural B.C.)
1 cup	brazil nuts (lightly toasted and chopped)

Base: Preheat the oven to 325°F.

Melt the butter. In a large bowl, combine the butter with the sugar, eggs, butterscotch chips, blackcurrants and liqueur. Stir well. In a smaller bowl, combine the flour, salt and baking powder. Stir the flour mixture into the butter mixture.

Spread the combined mixture in a greased baking pan 9 x 13 inches. Bake at 325°F for 30 to 40 minutes, until golden all over and Beginning to Brown just around the edges. Cool the pan on a rack. When the base is completely cool, top with the glaze.

Glaze: Mix the sugar, liqueur and water together well and spread over the base. Sprinkle the chopped Brazil nuts over the glaze.

Let glaze set before cutting into squares.

Star of Emma Cookies

Susan MacPhee

One of the most important people in my life is a seven-year-old girl named Emma Madden Krasnick. A couple of years ago I developed this recipe as a present for Emma to mark the first day of Hanukkah. It combines my mother's recipe for Scottish shortbread cookies with the Jewish tradition of almond cookies. It seemed important that Emma have a joining of both her antecedent cultures: Celtic and Jewish. Emma, her younger sister, Hannah, and her parents, Mary and Allan, all enjoy these cookies, as, no doubt, her new sister, Abbie, will. So do my partner, Sudsy, and I, and everyone else who happens to drop by over the holiday season.

Makes 4 dozen cookies

1 cup	butter, softened (not melted)
1 1/4 cups	ground blanched almonds
1/2 cup	icing sugar
1/2 cup	cornstarch
1 cup	unbleached white flour
1/2 tsp	salt

Preheat the oven to 350°F.

Cream the butter and ground almonds together until fluffy. Combine the icing sugar, cornstarch, flour and salt in a sifter and sift onto the butter mixture. Continue to cream until everything is well combined and it's obvious that the dough will hold together. Form it into a ball and, on a lightly floured surface, roll it out to about 1/2 inch thick. With a round cutter about 1 1/2 inches in diameter, cut out the cookies—there should be 3 dozen round cookies. I also make a dozen 1-inch star-shaped cookies for Emma.

Bake the round cookies at 350°F on an ungreased cookie sheet for 12 to 15 minutes. The stars, being smaller, will take 10 minutes at most.

Mom's Sugar Cookies

Karen Stewart

We always had wonderful Christmas trees when I was growing up. My mother made Christmas extra special by filling the tree with colourful, festive decorations. These decorations never seemed to last too long, though, since they were hard to resist. They were individually wrapped Santas, bells, snowmen, stars, snowflakes and more: all of them cookies. I have carried on this tradition, although I don't make nearly as many cookies as my mother did, much to my children's dismay.

Makes approximately 80 cookies

1 cup	butter
1 cup	white sugar
1/4 cup	milk
1/2 tsp	vanilla
1	large egg, beaten (2 if small)
2 1/2 cups	flour
1/2 tsp	salt
2 tsp	baking powder

Cream the butter, then add the sugar gradually and cream well. Add the milk and vanilla to the beaten egg. Sift the flour, salt and baking powder together. Add the dry ingredients and the liquid ingredients alternately to the creamed mixture. Separate the dough in half, then chill it for 1 hour.

Preheat the oven to 375°F.

Roll out a small portion of the dough at a time to 1/4-inch thickness on a floured pastry cloth. Keep the remaining dough in the refrigerator and save all scraps after cutting for the final rolling so that the dough does not become overworked. Cut cookies with your favourite Christmas cookie cutters, place on a greased cookie sheet, and bake in a moderate oven (375°F) for 8 minutes.

When the cookies are cool, decorate them with coloured icing or leave them plain. These cookies are good either way.

Pepparkakor

Maja Grip

As air force brats, my siblings and I spent much of our childhood in France and Germany—a long way from British Columbia, where most of our relatives lived. My father's sister, Lucille, who lived in Youbou, sent us a box of these traditional Swedish cookies each Christmas. They didn't withstand the rigours of overseas mail very well and often arrived completely shattered—but we ate them anyway, and the spicy crumbs came to epitomize Christmas for us.

Pepparkakor (accent on the first and third syllables) remain part of my own Christmas tradition, and each year I make dozens to mail to family and friends. They are perfect companions for the good strong coffee favoured by those of us with Swedish or Finnish roots. And when they're in the oven, the delicious aroma evokes Christmas for me like nothing else.

Makes approximately 6 dozen cookies

1 cup	butter
1 1/2 cups	white sugar
1	egg
1 tbsp	finely chopped or grated fresh orange zest (choose an extra-fragrant orange)
2 tsp	corn syrup
1 tbsp	water
3 1/4 cups	flour
2 tsp	baking soda
1 tbsp	cinnamon
2 tsp	ginger
1 tsp	cloves
1/2 tsp	cardamom seeds, ground

Cream together the butter and sugar. Beat in the egg, orange zest, syrup and water. Sift together the flour, baking soda and spices, then add to the moist ingredients about a third at a time (the dough will become quite stiff, and you may need to use your hands to knead in the final third).

Divide the dough in four and pat each section into a flat disk. Wrap the disks individually in waxed paper or plastic wrap, then seal all four in a large freezer bag. Freeze for up to a month, or chill overnight in the fridge.

To bake the cookies, preheat the oven to 375°F.

Unwrap a dough disk and set it on a floured board at room temperature until it becomes slightly pliable. Roll out the dough very thin—about 1/8 inch thick—and cut it into festive shapes. Bake on a greased cookie sheet at 375°F for about 10 minutes. The cookies will puff up briefly and then subside, and they will colour slightly. Cool on a rack.

Pepparkakor will keep for many months in an airtight tin, but they seldom need to!

Grandma Bondi's Sicilian Honey Cakes

Pam Rietzler

In 1902 my grandfather, then twelve, emigrated with his family from Sicily to Chicago. He met my grandmother at a local carnival. She quickly became part of the Sicilian family—from learning how to speak Italian to becoming an excellent Italian cook. Every visit to their house was special, but Christmas day was really magical. When we arrived in the morning, my sister and I would peer into the downstairs bedrooms, where the beds were draped with crisp white linen sheets covered with homemade ravioli. After an afternoon of presents and snacks and drinks, it was dinnertime. There were never fewer than thirty of us.

I remember the day I was old enough to graduate from eating in the kitchen to eating at the main dining table. The table was set with Grandma's finest china and silver, with wine glasses for every course . . .

After the ravioli, Grandpa would come out with a huge turkey that he ceremoniously carved at the table. My eyes were also on the sideboard, where the honey cookies sat on a large silver tray. After dinner dishes were cleared (it seemed my Aunt Rosalie washed dishes for hours), it was dessert time. We would have a bowl of mixed nuts to crack, a bowl of fruit (lots of grapes and figs) and these Honey Cakes. They were marvellous!

Makes 12 to 16 cookies

4	egg yolks
1 tbsp	butter, melted
1 cup	flour
1/2 tsp	baking powder
1 tbsp	sugar
1/2 tsp	cinnamon
2 tbsp	water
	oil or vegetable shortening for deep frying
	honey
	icing sugar

Beat the egg yolks with the melted butter. In a separate bowl, sift together the flour, baking powder, sugar and cinnamon. Add the dry ingredients and 2 tbsp water alternately to the egg mixture (add more water if the dough is too stiff).

Knead the dough until it is firm and smooth, then roll out as thin as for noodles (a pasta machine works well for this). Cut the dough into strips about 1/2 inch wide and 6 inches long, and either twist them into figure-8 shapes or leave them as strips.

Fry the cookies in hot oil and drain them on paper towels. When cool, drizzle with warm honey and sprinkle with icing sugar. This recipe can also be doubled.

Uncle Wiggly Squares

Yvette Brend

This is not a low-fat recipe! You have to understand that this is a recipe born of a childhood in the seventies. And you have to understand the context. When Mr. Main retired from Doncaster Elementary after forty years, the students wanted to give him a present. So we created a cookbook, Doncaster's "Main" Course. Get it? We were ten-year-olds, okay! Each section was illustrated with a student sketch. This recipe can be found in the "Cakes, Cookies and Squares" segment—introduced by a rumpled-looking Cookie Monster with extra-googly eyes. But the real significance of this square is the chef who made them most. Mrs. Marilyn Moody was the neighbourhood mother where I grew up at the end of the Cedar Hill Golf course. On birthdays and every other occasion (happy or sad), she always showed up laden with baking and smiling that huge Mrs. Moody smile. And she still does it—thirty years later. She has kept track of every child who went to school or played with the Moody kids (all four of them, including the twins—Wayne, Wendy, Deanna and Jennifer). We swear she has a map of the world with pins in it to keep track of us all. I can still hear her calling in the clan from the tire swing. But she never had to call long if the promise was "Uncle Wiggly Squares."

So here it is ... manna from heaven that was always hot and fresh in the Moody kitchen.

Makes 16 squares

1/2 cup	margarine
3/4 cup	brown sugar
2 cups	oatmeal
1/2 tsp	vanilla
1/4 tsp	almond extract

Preheat the oven to 350°F.

Melt the margarine and add the sugar, oatmeal, vanilla and almond extract. Press the mixture into an ungreased 8-inch square pan.

Bake at 350°F for 15 minutes.

Ester's Spritz Cookies

Bonna and Rob Dawson

Here is my favourite cookie recipe. It was copied from a magazine or newspaper recipe many years ago, so I cannot provide an accurate source. I have changed the method of forming the cookies, so I suppose it is my recipe now. These always remind me of childhood Christmas preparations. Similar cookies were made by my mother, eventually with my help and that of my brother and sister, and put away to be served on Christmas day. Surplus cookies were served at the various family dinners that took place throughout the season, and we kids certainly looked forward to eating them. These melt in your mouth, and one is never enough.

It took me a few years to find a cookie press of my own, one with the designs and nozzles that I wanted. I persevered, however, and it was worth the hunt. Over the years, my three daughters have enjoyed helping to make these cookies, and who knows, perhaps they will pass on this recipe, and the fun involved, to their children!

Makes 7 dozen cookies

2 cups	sifted flour
1 tsp	baking powder
1/8 tsp	salt
1 cup	butter, softened
3/4 cup	white sugar
1	egg yolk, unbeaten
1 tsp	almond extract
	glacé cherries for decoration

Sift together the flour, baking powder and salt. With a mixer, cream the butter and gradually add the sugar, beating until very light and fluffy. Add the egg yolk and almond extract, beating until well blended. With the mixer on low speed, gradually add in the flour mixture, beating just until well mixed. Wrap in waxed paper and refrigerate for half an hour or until the dough is easy to handle.

Preheat the oven to 350°F.

Place the dough in a cookie press fitted with the zigzag or Christmas tree shaper. Using cold, ungreased cookie sheets, form the shapes to fill the sheets. Cut small slices of glacé cherries and place one slice on each cookie. Press it down slightly with your fingertip to secure it to the dough.

Bake the cookies at 350°F for 8 to 10 minutes. Their edges should just be light gold—do not overbake. (CBC baker's note: Keep a close eye on them— they will burn in the time it takes to wash a measuring cup!) Cool on a wire rack.

Store in a tightly closed container or wrapped in foil. Can be refrigerated for up to 2 weeks.

Caramel Bars

Shelley Hardcastle

When I was in grade 12, I had a good friend who was attending the University of Victoria. One weekend, another friend and I convinced our parents to let us go on a road trip to visit her. The mother of our university friend put together a care package for her daughter. As we rolled along the highway, heading for the ferry, we got a bit peckish. We peeked into the care package, found some of these Caramel Bars and thought we might sneak just one. Then another, and another. Of course, we saved one for our friend at university. Upon returning home, I had to phone her mom to get this recipe. Unfortunately my friend's mom and I are no longer in touch, but I remember her fondly every time I pull out the recipe, now wrinkled, torn and smudged.

Makes 24 large bars

Bottom layer

1 cup	butter
2 cups	flour
1/2 cup	sugar
1 1/2 tsp	vanilla

Middle layer

1 cup	butter
1 cup	brown sugar
4 tbsp	corn syrup
1 can	sweetened condensed milk (300 mL)

Top layer

1 cup	chocolate chips
1 cup	butterscotch chips

Bottom layer: Preheat the oven to 325°F. Combine all of the ingredients for the bottom layer and press into a greased pan 9 x 13 inches. Bake at 325°F for 30 minutes.

Middle layer: Cook all of the ingredients in a double boiler, stirring occasionally, until thick. Pour over the bottom layer. Cool slightly.

Top layer: Melt the chocolate and butterscotch chips together and pour over the bottom two layers.

Cut into 24 piggy-sized bars, or cut into more dainty bars and then eat twice as many.

Try to save some for your friends!

Brown-Eyed Susans

Lois J. Richardson

This recipe has been passed down through my husband's family. My mother-in-law gave it to me twenty-five years ago, when I was dating her son.

    I bake these cookies only on special occasions, not because they are difficult to make but because once they are made I can't stop eating them. They seem to have the same effect on everyone who tastes them. People rave about these cookies, and I have never been left with anything but an empty plate when I serve them.

Makes 3 dozen cookies

1 cup	butter
3 tbsp	sugar
1 tsp	almond extract
2 cups	flour
1/2 tsp	salt

Icing

1 cup	icing sugar, sifted
2 tbsp	unsweetened cocoa powder
2 tbsp	hot water
1/2 tsp	vanilla
	almond halves for decorating the cookies

Preheat the oven to 400°F.

Cream the butter, then add the sugar, almond extract, flour and salt. Roll level tablespoons of this mixture into balls. Place the balls on a greased cookie sheet and flatten slightly.

Bake at 400°F for 12 to 15 minutes. Cool, then ice.

Icing: Combine the icing sugar and cocoa. Add the water and vanilla. Put 1/2 tsp of icing on each cookie, pressing an almond half into the centre.

Butter Tart Squares

Clo Carey

"Squares are always a good standby," my cousin told me. Having grown up in Ireland on a steady diet of tea brack and soda bread with jam, I hadn't a clue what she was talking about. But I was willing to try anything once. "You can bake them ahead and freeze them on platters," my cousin said. "Defrost them the morning of the party and you're all set." The "ahead" bit appealed to me. I was a full-time student, working part-time and four months pregnant. Somehow feeling my status as superwoman was still in jeopardy, I was convinced that a dessert party for everyone my husband and I had ever known was the answer.

I planned my campaign and researched my recipes. Day after day the oven spewed out trayloads of goodies and the freezer gobbled them up. Despite the fact that I had sufficient supplies to feed an army, one more type of square seemed crucial to the success of the enterprise. I scanned the index of an aunt's church cookbook: lemon squares, got those; coconut squares, check; brownies, done. Butter Tart Squares—now those sounded different. Into the oven they went.

The great day dawned. I removed my platters of prepared goodies from the freezer and arranged as many as I could on the dining room table. The rear guard were left defrosting all over the house. I went off to kick any lingering clutter into cupboards and transform myself into a hostess. Much later, as I was tossing chopped fruit into the mulled wine, I heard a noise in the dining room. One glance through the door and my stomach hit my boots. There was our cat, Monty, a white shaggy-haired affair, up on the table, delicately licking the tops off all my lovely squares. To say I let out a bellow would be to understate the ferocity of the sound. I have never seen a cat disappear into thin air so fast.

Close inspection of the treats revealed little raspy tongue marks on all but the Butter Tart Squares. Were they terrible, or did the cat just not like raisins? In a panic I stuffed one into my mouth. It was delicious. As I hastily removed the polluted platters and replaced them with the reserves from around the house, I crammed another Butter Tart Square into my mouth. Heaven!

Despite the spread being a little thinner than I had hoped, the party was a great hit, and so were the Butter Tart Squares. Over the years, I have trotted them out for every festive occasion. As I watch them bubble in the oven, I am always reminded of our very naughty cat, who sadly is no longer with us.

**Makes approximately
3 dozen squares**

Base

¹/₂ cup	*margarine*
1 cup	*flour*
2 tbsp	*brown sugar*

Topping

2	*eggs*
1¹/₂ cups	*brown sugar*
¹/₂ cup	*oatmeal*
¹/₄ tsp	*salt*
¹/₂ tsp	*baking powder*
1 tsp	*vanilla*
¹/₂ cup	*raisins, currants, or chopped walnuts or pecans*

Preheat the oven to 350°F.

Base: Melt the margarine, and then mix it with the flour and the 2 tbsp brown sugar. Press into a greased 9-inch square pan. Bake at 350°F for 15 minutes, until a very light brown.

Topping: Beat the eggs together until blended. Mix them and the rest of the topping ingredients together well, and pour the mixture over the partially baked base. Bake again for 20 minutes.

Cool and cut into squares. Recipe can be doubled.

Adapted from a recipe submitted by Donna Wheeler to *Bless This Food,* a cookbook published by Leaside Presbyterian Church, Toronto.

Molasses Cookies

Cathy Hunt

While my little sister was busy getting married, her new in-laws were busy collecting recipes from present and past generations to create a most unique wedding gift, a family cookbook. *Susie & Simon's Family Cookbook* is full of great tales and recipes, similar to this cookbook. My step-sister, Heather Kimmie, contributed this favourite down-east Nova Scotia cookie recipe.

Makes 2 to 3 dozen cookies

1 cup	sugar
3/4 cup	shortening
1	egg
1/4 cup	molasses
2 tsp	baking soda
2 cups	flour, sifted
1/2 tsp	salt
1/2 tsp	cloves
1/2 tsp	ginger
1 tsp	cinnamon
	white sugar to dip cookies into

Preheat the oven to 350°F.

Mix the ingredients in the order listed. Form the dough into balls. Dip the tops into white sugar, place on a greased cookie sheet, flatten slightly.

Bake at 350°F for 8 to 10 minutes.

Recipe Testing

All of the recipes in this book have been carefully tested by our wonderful test team: chef Tara Molloy, who jumped in at the last moment and tested twenty-five of the recipes during a rare Vancouver heat wave, and chef and instructor Nathan Hyam, instructor Robert Nicholson and the students from the Riverside Secondary School Culinary Arts program and Home Economics department in Richmond, British Columbia, who expertly put all the other recipes through their paces.

Riverside's Culinary Arts program is aimed at grade 11 and 12 students who are planning a career in the restaurant industry. It provides hands-on training in a commercial kitchen, and the students produce all the food for their school cafeteria, serving breakfast and lunch to about 400 fellow students a day. Their goal is to serve natural food made from scratch. Reflecting the diversity of the school population, Riverside students prepare Chinese, Thai, Vietnamese, Italian, French, Mexican, Greek and Canadian homestyle cuisines.

The Riverside student team was Amanda Lynn Pynn, Jessica Ladan, Katie Carson, April Knoll, Jeff Wong, Mike Vaclavik, Meagan Jewell, Aaron Grant, Renee Morwick, Lindsey Allan, Michelle Arthur, Travis Collier, Kristen Gibeault, Brittany Goldhawke, Diego Guzman, Mike Hargrave, Sasha Jamile, Colin Jones, Natasha Kaloya, Tom Ling, Adam Liu, Angela Mackie, Nicole McAdam, Sheliza Mohamed, Sarah Morissette and Krystal Richard.

Recipe Conversions

The following equivalents may be used to convert recipes in this book to metric measurements.

Volume

1/8 tsp	0.5 mL
1/4 tsp	1 mL
1/3 tsp	2 mL
1/2 tsp	2.5 mL
1 tsp	5 mL
1/2 tbsp	7.5 mL
1 tbsp	15 mL
1/4 cup	50 mL
1/3 cup	75 mL
1/2 cup	125 mL
2/3 cup	150 mL
3/4 cup	175 mL
1 cup	250 mL

Oven temperatures

300°F	150°C
325°F	160°C
350°F	175°C
375°F	190°C
400°F	205°C
425°F	220°C

Length

1/8 inch	3 mm
1/4 inch	6 mm
1/2 inch	13 mm
3/4 inch	19 mm
1 inch	25 mm

Baking pans and sheets

8-inch square	20 x 20 cm
9-inch square	22 x 22 cm
7 x 11 inches	18 x 28 cm
8 x 10 inches	20 x 25 cm
9 x 13 inches	22 x 33 cm
10 x 15 inches	25 x 38 cm
11 x 17 inches	28 x 43 cm
12 x 18 inches	30 x 45 cm

Weight

3 oz	85 g
4 oz	125 g
1/8 lb	57 g
1/4 lb	125 g
1/2 lb	250 g
3/4 lb	375 g
1 lb	500 g

Index